D1549690

Mixer and Blender COOKBOOK

Myra Street

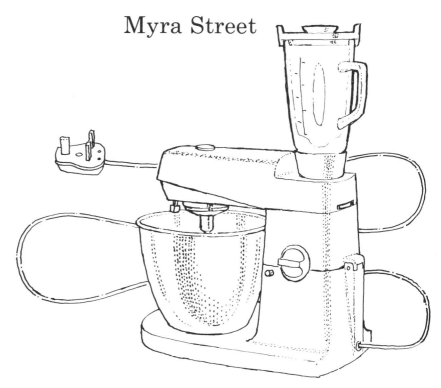

HAMLYN

London · New York · Sydney · Toronto

Contents

Published by
The Hamlyn Publishing Group Limited
London · New York · Sydney · Toronto
Astronaut House, Feltham, Middlesex, England
© Copyright 1972 The Hamlyn Publishing Group Limited
First published 1972
Sixth impression 1977
ISBN 0 600 36057 1
Filmset by Photoprint Plates Limited, Rayleigh, Essex
Printed by Chapel River Press, Andover, England
Cover photograph by Roy Rich, Angel Studios
Line drawings by Gay John Galsworthy

ACKNOWLEDGEMENTS
The author and publishers thank the following
for their co-operation in supplying photographs
for this book:

Bosch Limited: page 12
Cadbury Schweppes Foods Limited Food Advisory Service:
pages 51, 59, 60
Carnation Milk Bureau: page 76
Fruit Producers' Council: cover, page 48
General Foods Limited: page 55
John West Foods Limited: pages 23, 46, 63
New Zealand Lamb Information Bureau: page 31
Pasta Foods Limited: pages 19, 35
Philips Electrical Limited: page 69
The Malayan Pineapple Industry Board: page 27
The Tupperware Company: page 17
Trex Cookery Service (J. Bibby Foods Products Limited):
page 65
Dishes and accessories used in the photography kindly
lent by David Mellor, Ironmonger, 4 Sloane Square,
London SW1W 8EE, and Harvey Nichols, Knightsbridge,
London SW1X 7RJ.

Introduction

Mixers and blenders have come to stay. These invaluable aids fulfill a very definite need for today's busy housewife. Perhaps you own a mixer and blender and feel a little guilty at the thought that it spends too much time in a cupboard, gathering dust and taking up precious space. This book will show you how to make the fullest possible use of two very useful pieces of equipment which are not luxuries but essential requirements for the modern kitchen.

A blender is an incredibly versatile machine, a secret weapon in the kitchen which no cook can really afford to be without–particularly anyone who wants to cook with a minimum of effort. When using a blender you may have to bend some of the basic rules of cookery–yet this adds interest to the whole culinary art.

I have friends who say that nothing would induce them to use the blender for making mayonnaise mainly because they enjoy standing in the kitchen with an oil dripper, stirring in the sauce. A soothing and satisfying occupation, agreed. But with a blender you can save yourself ten minutes in which to sit down and relax–even more soothing and satisfying to the working hostess.

The blender is marvellous for giving you a variety of gourmet dishes at the flick of a switch–pâtés, pâté terrines, sauces, stuffings, and sweets–which would take so much longer using conventional methods.

If you use your mixer and blender in conjunction with other labour-saving equipment, time which would otherwise be spent in shopping or in the kitchen can be spent with the family. Remember to plan ahead. Several dishes can be cooked overnight in the automatic oven to save you long cooking sessions for several days. ✤ Again, if you have a home freezer, you can use your blender to take a lot of the effort out of cooking food in large quantities.

The blender can also help you save on food bills. All those odd little pieces that you hoard in plastic boxes can be made into sandwich fillings; leftover vegetables can be made into quick soups. Commercial convenience foods can be duplicated in your own kitchen–particularly those for babies and toddlers.

All in all, how did you ever live without your mixer and blender? Expensively? With these useful kitchen aids cookery becomes less arduous and as a bonus you may even find yourself saving money.

Myra Street

Note: Next to every recipe title is a symbol. This is to show you at a glance which piece of equipment you will need–a mixer, a blender, or both. In some recipes, for example in the meat section, the symbol refers to the mixer or blender needed to make the pastry or stuffing, to prepare an ingredient for use in the recipe, or to make a suggested accompaniment. The symbols are:

mixer

blender

mixer and blender

The star symbol ✤ throughout the text is used to indicate a hint on freezing for freezer owners, and helps to identify quickly recipes which freeze well.

USEFUL FACTS AND FIGURES

Metric measures

In converting recipes from Imperial measures to their metric equivalents, we recommend that solids and liquids should be taken to the nearest number of grammes and millilitres which is divisible by 25. If the nearest unit of 25 gives scant measure the liquid content in a recipe must also be reduced. For example, in the chart below you will see that 1 oz. is 28 g. when rounded off to the nearest whole figure but only 25 g. when rounded off to the nearest unit of 25.

Ounces/fluid ounces	Approx. g. and ml. to nearest whole figure	Recommended conversion to nearest unit of 25
1	28	25
2	57	50
3	85	75
4	113	100
5 ($\frac{1}{4}$ pint)	142	150
6	170	175
7	198	200
8 ($\frac{1}{2}$ lb.)	226	225
9	255	250
10 ($\frac{1}{2}$ pint)	283	275
11	311	300
12	340	350
13	368	375
14	396	400
15 ($\frac{3}{4}$ pint)	428	425
16 (1 lb.)	456	450
17	484	475
18	512	500
19	541	550
20 (1 pint)	569	575

Note: When converting quantities over 20 oz. first add the appropriate figures in the centre column, *then* adjust to the nearest unit of 25.

Oven temperature chart

	Fahrenheit	Celsius	Gas Mark
Very cool	225	110	$\frac{1}{4}$
	250	130	$\frac{1}{2}$
Cool	275	140	1
	300	150	2
Moderate	325	170	3
	350	180	4
Moderately hot	375	190	5
	400	200	6
Hot	425	220	7
	450	230	8
Very hot	475	240	9

The Celsius (formerly Centigrade) equivalents are the temperatures recommended by the Electricity Council.

Notes for American users

In the recipes in this book the ingredients are given in American standard cup measures as well as in Imperial measures. The list below gives some American equivalents or substitutes for terms used in the book.

British	American
Baked/unbaked pastry case	Baked/unbaked pie shell
Baking tin	Baking pan
Cocktail stick	Wooden toothpick
Cake mixture	Batter
Deep cake tin	Spring form pan
Frying pan	Skillet
Greaseproof paper	Wax paper
Grill	Broil/Broiler
Kitchen paper	Paper towels
Mixer/Liquidiser	Mixer/Blender
Muslin	Cheesecloth
Pastry cutters	Cookie cutters
Patty tins	Muffin pans/cups
Piping bag	Pastry bag
Pudding basin	Pudding mold/ovenproof bowl
Sandwich tin	Layer cake pan
Stoned	Pitted
Swiss roll tin	Jelly roll pan
Whisk	Whip/beat

Note: The British pint is 20 fluid ounces as opposed to the American pint which is 16 fluid ounces.

Notes for Australian users

Ingredients in this book are given in both cup measures and in pounds and ounces. The old Australian standard measuring cup is the same as the American standard 8-fluid ounce cup; the new Australian cup is bigger and holds 250 ml. It is most important to remember that the Australian tablespoon differs from both the British and American tablespoon; the table below gives a comparison between the standard tablespoons used in the three countries. A teaspoon holds approximately 5 millilitres in all three countries; the British standard tablespoon holds 17·7 millilitres, the American 14·2 millilitres, and the Australian 20 millilitres.

British	American	Australian
1 teaspoon	1 teaspoon	1 teaspoon
1 tablespoon	1 tablespoon	1 tablespoon
2 tablespoons	3 tablespoons	2 tablespoons
3$\frac{1}{2}$ tablespoons	4 tablespoons	3 tablespoons
4 tablespoons	5 tablespoons	3$\frac{1}{2}$ tablespoons

All cup and spoon measures in this book are level.

Mixers

There are many types of mixer available to the housewife today and each type can be ideal for different family needs.

Before choosing a mixer it is wise to consider the growth or declining size of the family, the amount of use the machine will have, and the reason for the purchase. Many people buy mixers only to save time and effort with cooking whereas others want them to extend the range of their meals as well as saving work. Although any type of mixer is a great help in the kitchen it is obviously useful for the woman with several children to have a large machine with a stand to enable larger quantities to be made up at one time. A small hand mixer is ideal for cooking for one or two although many people prefer them to the larger stand models because it is possible to use them for beating and mixing in any bowl or pan. Small mixers can be used by holding in the hand or, for most models, a stand may be purchased.

Many people buy the mixer first and then return for the stand and some of the extras which are available. Several small models have extras such as slicers, shredders, coffee mills, and juice extractors as well as stands and bowls. Before buying a hand mixer do try to have a demonstration and see if it feels comfortable to use.

Before buying a table model, make sure you can find it a permanent home on a stable surface. This piece of machinery is too heavy to heave in and out of a cupboard. People who keep mixers tucked away in a cupboard seldom use them for this reason.

Once you have decided on buying a mixer, make up your mind that it's going to earn its living. It is essential to have a demonstration before you buy. Then you can see how the machine is assembled, how it is used, and how the beaters are removed. This is most important as some manufacturers have not yet learned how to explain themselves to people like me who do not have a mind for things mechanical. Don't be like a friend of mine who confessed that she had to slip a bowl full of soapy water under the beaters to wash them as she couldn't work out how to remove them!

Your choice of machine will be a matter of personal preference and needs. But there are several golden rules to remember when buying a mixer which apply to both large and small.

1. Buy a machine which is adequate for the amount of use it will have. A cheaper, lighter one is not always a bargain if you intend to use it for heavy beating.
2. Make sure that it is easy to clean. Machines with blenders attached sometimes have bases which do not unscrew and it makes cleaning difficult if any food catches round the blades.
3. Read the manual supplied with the machine and follow the manufacturer's instructions if you want to obtain the best results and prolong the life of the machine. Most mixers and blenders need very little servicing.
4. Make sure any attachment which can be bought with your machine is really worth the space in the kitchen cupboard.
5. Read the recipe leaflet supplied with your mixer and use the correct speeds for similar recipes.

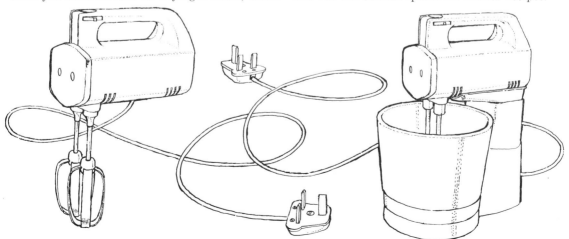

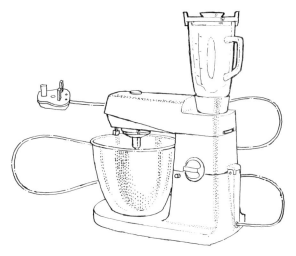

Attachments

The following attachments are available with many mixers.

Can opener I really could not be bothered to fix a can opener onto my mixer for the occasional can but a friend of mine finds it well worth while for opening the cans of dog and cat food which her menagerie of pets consume.

Shredder This is useful for soups and vegetables but I find my blender is much easier to use for crumbs, nuts, and coarsely chopping vegetables.

Coffee grinder If you grind your own coffee, you could use a blender. But the strong flavour of the coffee often lingers on. So it's best to use a coffee grinder.

Juice extractor Marvellous for health food addicts who want vegetable and fruit juices. I think it's a bother washing it afterwards unless you're going to extract pints at a time.

Mincer Thoroughly recommended to those who hang on to leftovers. With the mincer you can transform left-over meat and vegetables into delicious savouries. ❄ If you own a home freezer the mincer is invaluable for making fresh hamburgers out of stewing meat. A hamburger tastes all the better for being freshly ground.

Sausage fillers can also be bought with the mincer. So if you can get hold of sausage skins, you're all set for homemade sausage production. Personally, I'm prepared to leave this pursuit to people who wistfully hark back to the days when sausages really had a taste!

Bean slicer and pea huller Very useful if you have a large garden planted out with lots of beans and peas–especially if you want to prepare them for the freezer.

Dough hook Essential if you are baking with yeast. It takes care of all the heavy kneading.

Cleaning mixers and attachments

Keep your mixer clean by washing over with a damp cloth and then drying with a clean towel. Removable parts may be washed in warm soapy water and then rinsed in cold water. Do not use scouring powders on the metal parts.

Wash attachments as soon as possible after use to avoid staining from vegetables and fruit juices.

Do not dry parts in direct heat as plastic parts may warp.

DO NOT PUT ELECTRICAL PARTS IN WATER.

Hints for using the mixer

Creaming fat and sugar for cakes Lowest speed should be used to begin with, then increase the speed to about one fifth of the maximum speed of the machine, i.e., if your machine has 10 speeds continue on number 2.

Beating in the eggs At the same speed beat in the eggs one at a time.

Adding flour and fruit At this stage I feel that it is time for the mixer to give way to the human touch. I think it is safer to fold in your flour with a sharp edged metal spoon rather than take the risk of overbeating. However, if you are braver than I am you can reduce your speed to minimum and tip in all the flour. Switch on for a second, switch off and add fruit, again switch on only for a second.

Rubbing in fat to flour for cakes, scones, and pastry Cut the fat into the flour roughly and use minimum speed until fat is rubbed in to the fine breadcrumb stage. Beware of leaving your machine on at this stage as it will form a dough without liquid if allowed to go past the fine breadcrumb stage.

Beating egg whites for meringues Maximum speed is used until egg whites are stiff and fluffy.

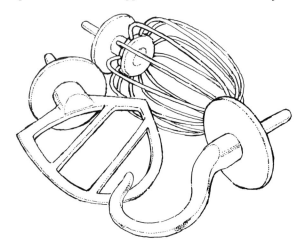

Blenders

The blender is an extremely versatile piece of equipment which opens up new avenues to the ambitious cook. Dishes which take hours of preparation without a blender suddenly come within range. Here are a few points to consider before making your purchase.

1. A small blender, though useful for most grinding and chopping tasks, will only take a small amount of mixture at a time. Do not run beyond the times recommended by the manufacturers. You'll need to be patient and work with small quantities when making soups, stuffings, and sweets.

2. Whichever blender you choose, make sure it is easy to clean. Some won't unscrew, making it difficult to clean properly underneath the blades.

3. Find out the capacity of the goblet. If you fill it too full, you're liable to have your kitchen sprayed!

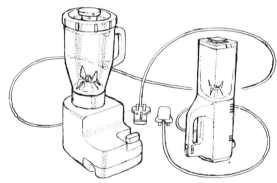

Cleaning the blender

Half fill with hot water and a drop of washing up liquid. Turn on to maximum speed for a few seconds. Empty the goblet and rinse. Use the same rules as you would for washing dishes. Rinse the blender first with cold water if it has been used for meat or egg mixtures which tend to turn solid in contact with hot water.

Hints for using the blender

With a well-stocked basic store cupboard it is amazing how you can make your own ingredients for cooking. In this direction, I am always finding new uses for my blender and getting out of a tricky spot when the shops are closed. Here are some of them.

Making castor sugar or icing sugar from granulated Put the granulated sugar into the goblet, not too much at a time, and run for a few seconds: until finely powdered for the castor sugar; until a dust for icing sugar.

Grating cheese Pop cubes of hard cheese into the blender a few at a time and grate until fine, using a medium speed (about 4). For this I usually wait until I have a few end pieces of cheese which are at the mousetrap stage. I then have a short grating session which keeps me going for sandwich spreads and sprinkling on top of finished dishes, like spaghetti and cauliflower. Store the grated cheese in an airtight plastic box in the fridge.

Chopping nuts Chop them finely or coarsely as the recipe demands, by popping in about 2 oz. at a time, using a medium speed. You can also make ground almonds from whole ones.

Making fresh breadcrumbs Done in a trice! This banishes one of the most time-consuming operations in the kitchen without a blender. You can make as much as you like without effort for coatings and stuffings.

Make rice into flour Handy since rice flour is difficult to find in grocers'. I like to use it in shortbread.

Grinding biscuits and cornflakes For flan cases, toppings, etc.

Making mayonnaise Use all the ingredients at room temperature and mayonnaise is yours in just a few seconds.

Making endless variety of salad dressings Only beware of leaving the machine on too long or the oil will emulsify.

Rescuing sauces with lumps You're saved with the flick of a switch!

Chopping herbs Wash and drain well before you start. ✳ I chop enough to store in the fridge or freezer in small plastic boxes and do enough herbs to last through the winter. You may need to add a little water to the herbs when chopping. Remember to drain well afterwards.

Sieving flour Literally in a second.

Grating citrus rinds Without grating your finger nails!

Making candied peel Feed through pieces about an inch long and do 4 oz. at a time in a large goblet.

Rubbing fat into flour Use for pastry and store in a plastic bag or jar in the fridge until needed.

Appetisers and soups

Appetisers

There's quite a fashion these days for economical and informal entertaining, using dips, fondues, and pâtés served up with delicious crusty bread.

The dips are often served as a first course to a meal or with the drinks as the guests arrive. I find the latter an ideal arrangement when one is short of time. It also solves the problem of those hungry guests who arrive directly from work, having missed lunch, and who would otherwise fade away waiting for the main meal.

❈ Most appetisers and starters can be made well in advance and stored in the refrigerator or freezer until needed; both can then be garnished just before serving.

SALMON AND CUCUMBER DIP
Illustrated on page 63

IMPERIAL	AMERICAN
7-oz. can salmon	7-oz. can salmon
2 oz. cucumber	$\frac{1}{2}$ cup diced cucumber
1 teaspoon lemon juice	1 teaspoon lemon juice
1 tablespoon tomato purée	1 tablespoon tomato paste
salt	salt
freshly ground black pepper	freshly ground black pepper
$\frac{1}{4}$ pint double cream	$\frac{2}{3}$ cup whipping cream
to garnish:	**to garnish:**
slices cucumber	slices cucumber

Remove the bone and skin from the salmon and blend the flesh with the cucumber, lemon juice, tomato purée, and seasoning. When smooth add the whisked cream and fold in carefully. Turn into a bowl and decorate the edge with cucumber slices cut into quarters. Serve with crisp biscuits.

CHEESE AND PINEAPPLE DIP
Illustrated on page 63

IMPERIAL	AMERICAN
12-oz. can pineapple pieces	12-oz. can pineapple tidbits
1 lb. cottage cheese	2 cups cottage cheese
salt and pepper	salt and pepper
2 tablespoons chopped chives	3 tablespoons chopped chives

Drain the pineapple. Blend the fruit at low speed, then add the cottage cheese and continue to blend for a few seconds. Season and add the chives. Turn into a bowl and decorate with a few pieces of pineapple. Serve with small crisp biscuits.

ANCHOVY DIP

IMPERIAL	AMERICAN
1 small can anchovies	1 small can anchovies
juice of 1 lemon	juice of 1 lemon
8 tablespoons mayonnaise (see page 17)	$\frac{2}{3}$ cup mayonnaise (see page 17)
6 tablespoons double cream	$\frac{1}{2}$ cup whipping cream
$\frac{1}{4}$ small onion	$\frac{1}{4}$ small onion
several sprigs parsley	several sprigs parsley
4 oz. cream cheese	$\frac{1}{2}$ cup cream cheese
salt and pepper	salt and pepper

Blend the anchovies with the lemon juice and add the mayonnaise, cream, onion, and parsley. Stop for a second and make sure all the ingredients are blended by pushing them round with a spatula. Switch on at medium speed and add the cheese in small amounts. Blend until smooth. Serve with crisps or small biscuits.

TUNA DIP
Illustrated on page 63

IMPERIAL	AMERICAN
6 tablespoons mayonnaise (see page 17)	$\frac{1}{4}$ cup mayonnaise (see page 17)
7-oz. can tuna	7-oz. can tuna
dash Tabasco sauce	dash Tabasco sauce
1 tablespoon lemon juice	1 tablespoon lemon juice
salt	salt
freshly ground black pepper	freshly ground black pepper
2 tablespoons green olives	3 tablespoons green olives

Make the mayonnaise as directed on page 17. Blend the tuna with the mayonnaise until smooth. Flavour with Tabasco sauce, lemon juice, and seasoning. Slice the olives and fold into the tuna mixture. Serve in a bowl, with crisps and biscuits.

AVOCADO DIP

IMPERIAL	AMERICAN
3 avocado pears	3 avocados
5-fl. oz. carton sour cream	$\frac{1}{3}$ cup sour cream
salt and pepper	salt and pepper
few drops Tabasco sauce	few drops Tabasco sauce
juice of $\frac{1}{2}$ lemon	juice of $\frac{1}{2}$ lemon
1 small can shrimps	1 small can shrimp
to garnish:	**to garnish:**
shrimps	shrimp

Halve the avocado pears lengthwise, remove the stones, and scoop the flesh from the skin carefully. Put the flesh into the blender. Retain the skins if you wish to serve the dip in these. Add the cream, seasoning, Tabasco, and lemon juice. Put the top on the blender and blend at high speed until smooth. Add the drained can of shrimps and blend on low speed until the shrimps are chopped, but not pulverised, unless you prefer a completely smooth dip. I like to leave small pieces of shrimp throughout the mixture. Serve in a bowl, or pile back into the avocado skins, with the usual small biscuits. Decorate with whole shrimps if the dip is a party piece.

Variation

Use 6 tablespoons (U.S. $\frac{1}{2}$ cup) mayonnaise (see page 17) in place of the sour cream. For extra flavour $\frac{1}{2}$ teaspoon curry powder can be added to the mixture.

SHRIMP DIP

IMPERIAL	AMERICAN
8 oz. peeled shrimps	$1\frac{1}{3}$ cups peeled shrimp
pinch cayenne pepper	pinch cayenne pepper
2 tablespoons lemon juice	3 tablespoons lemon juice
5-fl. oz. carton sour cream	$\frac{2}{3}$ cup sour cream
$\frac{1}{2}$ cucumber	$\frac{1}{2}$ cucumber
salt and pepper	salt and pepper
to garnish:	**to garnish:**
shrimps	shrimp

Sprinkle the shrimps with the cayenne pepper and lemon juice and allow to stand for at least half an hour. Put the cream and the peeled and cubed cucumber into the blender and blend at high speed for a few seconds, until smooth. Add the shrimps and blend until smooth, season to taste. Garnish with whole shrimps and a sprinkling of cayenne pepper. Serve with small crisp biscuits.

TOMATO AND EGG DIP

IMPERIAL	AMERICAN
6 tomatoes	6 tomatoes
6 hard-boiled eggs	6 hard-cooked eggs
10 tablespoons mayonnaise (see page 17)	$\frac{3}{4}$ cup mayonnaise (see page 17)
1 teaspoon Worcestershire sauce	1 teaspoon Worcestershire sauce
salt and pepper	salt and pepper

Dip the tomatoes in boiling water, skin them, then blend the peeled tomatoes with the shelled hard-boiled eggs, mayonnaise, and seasoning. Serve in a small bowl. For extra flavour add $\frac{1}{2}$ teaspoon curry powder to the mixture.

Variation

Cut eggs in half lengthwise. Blend the yolks with the other ingredients and pile or pipe the mixture back into the egg whites.

CHEESY CHARLIES

IMPERIAL	AMERICAN
2 oz. suet	$\frac{1}{3}$ cup shredded suet
$\frac{1}{2}$ pint water	$1\frac{1}{4}$ cups water
2 oz. plain flour	$\frac{1}{2}$ cup all-purpose flour
2 eggs	2 eggs
2 oz. cheese	$\frac{1}{2}$ cup grated cheese
salt and cayenne pepper	salt and cayenne pepper
pinch dry mustard	pinch dry mustard

Melt the suet in a saucepan. Add the water and bring to the boil. Add the flour and beat thoroughly with a hand mixer until the mixture forms a ball and leaves the side of the pan clean. Remove from the heat, cool slightly, and gradually beat in the eggs. Grate the cheese in the blender; beat in the seasoning and cheese. Drop teaspoonfuls of the mixture into hot oil or fat and deep fry until golden brown. Drain on absorbent paper and serve hot. Serve on sticks with drinks.
Serves 4

Variation

Substitute 2 oz. (U.S. $\frac{1}{3}$ cup) chopped prawns for the cheese.

MOROCCAN STARTER

IMPERIAL	AMERICAN
¼ pint olive oil	⅔ cup olive oil
3 tomatoes	3 tomatoes
2–3 aubergines	2–3 eggplants
4–6 courgettes	4–6 small zucchini
½ small leek	½ small leek
few sprigs parsley	few sprigs parsley
½ teaspoon cumin	½ teaspoon cumin
½ teaspoon cayenne pepper	½ teaspoon cayenne pepper

Heat the oil in a heavy frying pan. Cut the tomatoes, aubergines, courgettes, and leek into ½-inch slices. Cook the vegetables in the oil, a few at a time, until they are tender. As they are cooked transfer to the blender and add the parsley and spices. Add a little of the cooking oil and blend on a medium speed. Do this in several batches and when all the mixture is blended return it to the pan with a little more oil and allow to cook until the oil is absorbed. Cut into portions, serve hot or cold. This starter can also be served as part of an hors d'œuvre.
Serves 6

TARAMASALATA

To make this recipe without a blender all the ingredients have to be chopped and then ground with a pestle and mortar. Using a blender, a time-consuming but delicious recipe becomes as simple to make as a sandwich filling! ❋ This mixture freezes well.

IMPERIAL	AMERICAN
1 medium-sized boiled potato	1 medium-sized boiled potato
1 clove garlic (optional)	1 clove garlic (optional)
8 oz. smoked cod's roe	½ lb. smoked cod's roe
juice of 1 lemon	juice of 1 lemon
few sprigs chopped parsley	few sprigs chopped parsley
2 tablespoons olive oil	3 tablespoons olive oil
to garnish:	**to garnish:**
lemon wedges or black olives	lemon wedges or ripe olives

Put the potato in the blender with the clove of garlic and switch on for a second. Add the cod's roe, lemon juice, and parsley and blend together. The mixture can now be treated rather like mayonnaise. Switch the blender on at a low speed. Add the oil drop by drop until the mixture is creamy. If the mixture becomes oily add a little more lemon juice.

Serve as a first course with hot buttered toast.
Serves 4

PRAWN AND CRAB COCKTAIL

IMPERIAL	AMERICAN
mayonnaise (see page 17)	mayonnaise (see page 17)
2 teaspoons tomato purée	2 teaspoons tomato paste
few drops Tabasco sauce	few drops Tabasco sauce
1 tablespoon whipped cream	1 tablespoon whipped cream
few drops brandy (optional)	few drops brandy (optional)
4 oz. prawns	⅔ cup peeled prawns
2 oz. crabmeat	¼ cup crabmeat
to garnish:	**to garnish:**
crisp green lettuce	crisp green lettuce
lemon twist	lemon twist
whole prawns	whole prawns

Combine the mayonnaise with the tomato purée, Tabasco, whipped cream, and brandy. Stir in the prawns and crabmeat. Tear the lettuce into strips and line the bottom of the glasses. Carefully spoon in the shellfish mixture and garnish each glass with a twist of lemon and a whole prawn in its shell if possible. A little chopped parsley may also be sprinkled over the top. Chill before serving but please do not make up the cocktails too far in advance otherwise the lettuce will be soggy and the whole effect will be spoiled.

Glass sweet dishes can be used but as they tend to be on the large side, most people serve this starter in ordinary wine glasses.
Serves 4

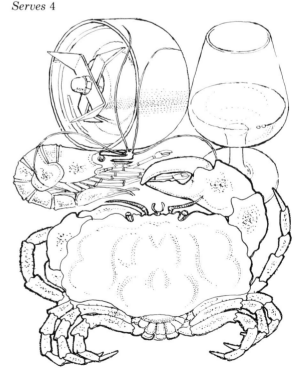

KIPPER STARTER

IMPERIAL	AMERICAN
8 oz. kipper fillets	½ lb. kipper fillets
juice of 1 lemon	juice of 1 lemon
2 tablespoons double cream	3 tablespoons whipping cream
salt and pepper	salt and pepper
2 oz. butter	¼ cup butter
to garnish:	**to garnish:**
chopped parsley	chopped parsley
lemon wedges	lemon wedges

Remove the skins from the kippers (or use canned fillets) and put the flesh into the blender; switch on at medium speed. Add the lemon juice and blend until smooth; add the cream and seasoning and blend for a few seconds. Remove the mixture to a mixing bowl and beat together with the softened butter, using a hand mixer or a wooden spoon, until the mixture is really creamy. ❀ Because of the extra washing up involved in mixing this I always make up at least three quantities of this recipe and freeze two as this recipe freezes well. Serve with hot buttered toast.
Serves 4

SAUSAGE SAVOURIES

IMPERIAL	AMERICAN
2 slices bread	2 slices bread
few sprigs parsley	few sprigs parsley
1 lb. sausagemeat	2 cups sausagemeat
1 teaspoon Worcestershire sauce	1 teaspoon Worcestershire sauce
1 tablespoon tomato ketchup	1 tablespoon tomato ketchup
salt and pepper	salt and pepper
to coat:	**to coat:**
1 egg	1 egg
fresh white breadcrumbs	fresh white bread crumbs

Break the bread into small pieces and drop into the blender. Switch on for a few seconds until fine breadcrumbs are formed. Remove onto a plate then chop the parsley in the blender. Mix the sausage-meat, chopped parsley, sauces, seasonings, and crumbs in a bowl. Break the egg and beat lightly. With lightly floured hands form the sausage mixture into small balls. Dip in the egg then into the crumbs. Fry in hot oil until golden brown. Serve on cocktail sticks with a tomato (see page 21) or mustard sauce.
Makes 30

Pâtés and terrines

Pâtés and terrines, served with thin toast or French bread, make delicious meal starters. The number of servings given here are for serving as a starter. If you want to serve a pâté as a light luncheon dish, or for a picnic in summer, you should allow twice the quantity to serve the same number of people.

❀ Pâtés freeze very well so several quantities may be made at once and the extra frozen. However, a better result is obtained if they are packed for the freezer in small portions rather than whole.

BACON AND LIVER PATE

IMPERIAL	AMERICAN
12 oz. streaky bacon	¾ lb. bacon
1 onion	1 onion
1 tablespoon flour	1 tablespoon flour
2 tablespoons milk	3 tablespoons milk
1 egg	1 egg
2 tablespoons sherry	3 tablespoons sherry
4 oz. chicken livers	¼ lb. chicken livers
½ teaspoon pepper	½ teaspoon pepper
1 teaspoon nutmeg	1 teaspoon nutmeg
½ teaspoon salt	½ teaspoon salt
7 oz. puff pastry	½-lb. pack frozen puff paste
beaten egg	beaten egg

Remove the rind and gristle from the bacon. Set aside six rashers and cut the rest into small pieces. Preheat the oven to 350°F., 180°C., Gas Mark 4. Put the onion, cut into eight pieces, into the goblet with the flour, milk, egg, and sherry. Run the blender on medium speed until the mixture is almost smooth. Add the chicken livers, chopped bacon, and seasoning gradually and blend until a smooth mixture is obtained. Line a 1-lb. loaf tin with the reserved bacon rashers. Pour the mixture into the tin and bake in a moderate oven for 40 minutes. Allow to cool for at least 10 minutes and then turn out of the tin. Brush over with beaten egg. Roll out 7 oz. of the puff pastry thinly in an oblong shape which will accommodate the loaf shaped mixture. Enclose the bacon and liver terrine in the pastry and seal the edges with beaten egg. Cut several slits across the top of the pastry to allow the steam to escape and decorate with rolled out pastry trimmings in the shape of leaves. Brush over with beaten egg and bake in a hot oven until golden brown.
Serves 6
Oven temperature pâté 350°F., 180°C., Gas Mark 4, pastry 425°F., 220°C., Gas Mark 7

1. Collect all the ingredients together. Line the bottom of an earthenware terrine or ovenproof dish with rashers of streaky bacon. Allow the ends to overlap the dish.

2. Put all the ingredients into the blender. Switch on at medium speed for a few seconds, stop and push ingredients towards the blades with a spatula. Switch on again for a few seconds. The mixture is ready when all ingredients have been pulverised into a smooth mixture. Turn into the dish and cover with the overlapping ends of the bacon.

3. When cooked, allow to cool, chill, then serve in the dish or turn out as shown in the picture. I think it is more easily sliced if turned out.

 TERRINE OF CHICKEN LIVERS

IMPERIAL	AMERICAN
2 oz. butter	$\frac{1}{4}$ cup butter
1 large onion	1 large onion
1 small clove garlic	1 small clove garlic
1 lb. chicken livers	1 lb. chicken livers
4 tablespoons chicken stock	$\frac{1}{3}$ cup chicken stock
salt and pepper	salt and pepper
2 eggs	2 eggs
4 tablespoons dry sherry	$\frac{1}{3}$ cup dry sherry
$\frac{1}{4}$ pint double cream	$\frac{2}{3}$ cup whipping cream
12–14 slices streaky bacon	12–14 slices bacon

Melt the butter in a frying pan and gently cook the roughly chopped onion, garlic, and chicken livers for a few minutes. Put into the blender with the stock, seasoning, eggs, and sherry. Blend at maximum speed until the mixture is smooth. Add the cream and blend for a few seconds. Line the terrine with the streaky bacon as shown in the picture. Pour in the mixture, cover, and cook for about 2 hours in a very moderate oven in a bain-marie, or water bath. I usually make a bain-marie to cook the terrine by putting an inch of water in my roasting tin.

Serves 6–8
Cooking time 2 hours
Temperature 325°F., 170°C., Gas Mark 3

 COUNTRY PATE

IMPERIAL	AMERICAN
8 oz. pig's liver	$\frac{1}{2}$ lb. pork liver
4 oz. chicken livers	$\frac{1}{4}$ lb. chicken livers
4 tablespoons white wine	$\frac{1}{3}$ cup white wine
1 clove garlic	1 clove garlic
1 egg	1 egg
4 tablespoons double cream	$\frac{1}{3}$ cup whipping cream
salt and freshly ground black pepper	salt and freshly ground black pepper
8 oz. belly of pork	$\frac{1}{2}$ lb. fresh picnic shoulder
2 bay leaves	2 bay leaves
8 slices streaky bacon	8 slices bacon

Cut the pig's liver into small pieces and put into the blender a little at a time with the chicken livers, wine, garlic, egg, cream, and seasoning. Mince the pork or cut it into small pieces and add to the mixture. Put into an earthenware bowl. Place the bay leaves on top and cover with the bacon. Cook uncovered in a slow oven, in a pan of water as directed in the preceding recipe, until the pâté comes away from the sides of the bowl. Serve with French bread or toast.

Serves 8
Cooking time 1½ hours
Temperature 300°F., 150°C., Gas Mark 2

Note: If you do not have a pâté dish or terrine improvise with a pyrex bowl or a 1- to 2-lb. loaf tin. This pâté improves with keeping.

SMOKED CHICKEN PATE

IMPERIAL	AMERICAN
8 oz. smoked chicken	½ lb. smoked chicken
rind of ½ lemon	rind of ½ lemon
juice of 1 lemon	juice of 1 lemon
1 tablespoon parsley	1 tablespoon parsley
salt	salt
freshly milled black pepper	freshly milled black pepper
¼ pint sour cream	⅔ cup sour cream
2 oz. butter	¼ cup butter
¼ pint aspic jelly	⅔ cup aspic jelly
(optional)	(optional)
to garnish:	**to garnish:**
sprigs watercress	sprigs watercress

Cut the smoked chicken into small pieces and put them into the blender. Switch on and run until the chicken is chopped. Peel the rind thinly from the lemon, add to the chicken with the juice, parsley, seasoning, and cream. Turn on at medium speed and add the butter gradually until a creamy mixture is obtained. Using a spatula put the mixture into six small ramekin dishes or one larger dish or bowl. If desired make up the aspic and spoon over the pâté just before the aspic is about to set.

Chill before serving and garnish with crisp watercress. Serve with toast or French bread. If you cannot get smoked chicken or turkey use roast poultry.
Serves 6

Fondue

Serving fondues with wine at parties is now very popular as it is a fairly economical way of entertaining. It also adds to the fun for everyone to help themselves. Many people are given fondue sets as gifts and I always think it is sad that many are only used as ornaments. Cheese fondue is delicious and easy to make; on page 32 you will see how to use the fondue set for beef.

Safety rules for fondue parties Do be careful with the little spirit burners which are supplied with the sets. Take care to place the fondue in a safe place so that people wielding their forks will not be likely to have accidents. A non-inflammable surface should be used as a base for the fondue stand, e.g., Formica. Don't put piles of paper napkins next to it. Please forgive my caution but it is so easy to overlook these small details in the enthusiasm of using your new fondue set.

SWISS FONDUE

IMPERIAL	AMERICAN
1 lb. Emmenthal cheese	1 lb. Emmenthal cheese
8 oz. Gruyère cheese	½ lb. Gruyère cheese
½ pint dry white wine	1¼ cups dry white wine
1 clove garlic	1 clove garlic
2 teaspoons salt	2 teaspoons salt
freshly grated nutmeg	freshly grated nutmeg
pinch cayenne pepper	pinch cayenne pepper
2–3 tablespoons Kirsch	3–4 tablespoons Kirsch
several French loaves	several French loaves

Cut the cheese into ½-inch cubes. Heat the wine slowly in a saucepan but do not allow it to boil. Pour into the goblet and add the clove of garlic and a few cheese cubes. Turn on at a low speed. Add the remainder of the cheese gradually. Blend until smooth, stopping to make sure all the cheese has been pushed towards the blades. Pour into a fondue pot or heavy saucepan and stir over the spirit burner of the fondue set or a low heat on the cooker until thick. Season and stir in the Kirsch. Cut the French bread into cubes. Using long forks dip the chunks of French bread into the fondue and eat as soon as it is cool enough.

Soups

Home-made soup is ideal for growing families. It helps to satisfy enormous appetites without stretching the family budget too much. The blender takes all the hard work out of making soups. Vegetables, meat, and chicken which sometimes accumulate in the refrigerator can be used by popping them in the blender and adding the purée to stock and milk.

Use the blender to add extra vegetables for flavour and quantity to canned and packet soups.

❋ Time and effort can be saved by making larger quantities and storing them in the refrigerator or home freezer. I have found some foil bags for sale in my local freezer shop which are ideal for storing soup.

For parties serve croûtons with your soups. Make these by deep frying dice or small triangles of bread until golden and crisp.

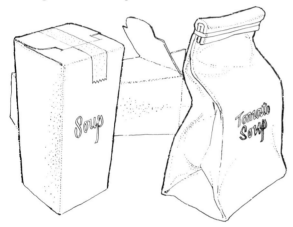

❄ AVOCADO SOUP

IMPERIAL	AMERICAN
1 large ripe avocado pear	1 large ripe avocado
1 clove garlic	1 clove garlic
$\frac{1}{2}$ pint milk	$1\frac{1}{4}$ cups milk
$\frac{1}{2}$ pint chicken stock	$1\frac{1}{4}$ cups chicken stock
salt and pepper	salt and pepper
$\frac{1}{4}$ pint sour cream	$\frac{2}{3}$ cup sour cream

Peel the avocado, cut in half, and remove the stone. Cut the flesh into four pieces and put into the blender goblet with the garlic, milk, chicken stock, and seasoning. Blend at maximum speed until smooth. Pour into a saucepan and heat, but do not boil. Stir in the sour cream just before serving. This is delicious served chilled with a garnish of sliced avocado.

❋ To freeze this soup, omit the cream and add just before reheating.
Serves 4

❄ VEGETABLE SOUP

IMPERIAL	AMERICAN
1 small onion	1 small onion
1 pint chicken or beef stock	$2\frac{1}{2}$ cups chicken or beef stock
1 carrot	1 carrot
1 turnip	1 turnip
1 stalk celery	1 stalk celery
3 sprigs parsley	3 sprigs parsley
$\frac{1}{4}$ pint single cream	$\frac{2}{3}$ cup coffee cream
salt and pepper	salt and pepper

Put the peeled and roughly chopped onion in the blender with about $\frac{1}{4}$ pint of the stock. Cover and blend for a few seconds. Gradually add the remaining vegetables, chopped, through the top, covering the hole before the machine is switched on. Put the puréed vegetables with the remaining stock into a saucepan and cook for 10 to 15 minutes. Pour the cream into the mixture before serving. This soup can also be served cold without any cooking.
Serves 4

Variation

Lentil soup Sauté all the roughly chopped vegetables in $1\frac{1}{2}$ oz. (U.S. 3 tablespoons) butter. Add 2 oz. (U.S. $\frac{1}{4}$ cup) washed lentils and the stock and simmer for $\frac{1}{2}$ hour. Put the soup into the blender about $\frac{3}{4}$ pint at one time. Reheat and serve. Stir in the cream before serving for cream of lentil soup.

❄ SPINACH SOUP

IMPERIAL	AMERICAN
1 lb. fresh spinach	1 lb. fresh spinach
outer leaves of a lettuce	outer leaves of a lettuce
3 spring onions	3 scallions
3 good sprigs parsley	3 good sprigs parsley
1 teaspoon chives	1 teaspoon chives
2 oz. butter	$\frac{1}{4}$ cup butter
salt and pepper	salt and pepper
$\frac{1}{2}$ teaspoon tarragon	$\frac{1}{2}$ teaspoon tarragon
$1\frac{1}{2}$ pints stock	$3\frac{3}{4}$ cups stock
$\frac{1}{4}$ pint single cream	$\frac{2}{3}$ cup coffee cream

Put the first five ingredients in the blender. Cover the vegetables with water, cover, and run on high speed until vegetables are finely chopped. Drain through a sieve. Melt the butter in a large saucepan, add sieved vegetables and seasoning, and sauté for a few minutes. Add the stock and cook for 15 to 20 minutes. Stir in the cream before serving.
Serves 6

POTATO AND LEEK SOUP

IMPERIAL	AMERICAN
1 lb. potatoes	1 lb. potatoes
2 onions	2 onions
2 oz. butter	$\frac{1}{4}$ cup butter
2 pints stock	5 cups stock
1 teaspoon chervil	1 teaspoon chervil
salt and pepper	salt and pepper
$\frac{1}{2}$ lb. leeks	$\frac{1}{2}$ lb. leeks
$\frac{1}{4}$ pint sour cream	$\frac{2}{3}$ cup sour cream
to garnish:	**to garnish:**
chopped spring onions	chopped scallions

Peel the potatoes and cut into rough slices. Chop the onions roughly, melt the butter in the soup pot, and sauté the potatoes with the onions for a few minutes. Add the stock, seasonings, and leeks and simmer until the potatoes are tender. Allow to cool slightly, mix with the sour cream, and put the soup through the blender at maximum speed. Serve hot or cold garnished with the finely chopped green spring onion tops.
Serves 4

Variation

Vichyssoise Substitute 1 pint (U.S. $2\frac{1}{2}$ cups) milk for 1 pint stock in the recipe and use double cream in place of sour cream. After the mixture is blended without the cream, return to the saucepan and simmer for 20 minutes, add the cream, and serve well chilled, garnished with chopped chives.

LETTUCE SOUP

IMPERIAL	AMERICAN
1 lb. potatoes	1 lb. potatoes
1 pint stock	$2\frac{1}{2}$ cups stock
salt and pepper	salt and pepper
1 large lettuce	1 large lettuce
1 pint milk	$2\frac{1}{2}$ cups milk
2 teaspoons chervil	2 teaspoons chervil
$1\frac{1}{2}$ oz. butter	3 tablespoons butter
4 tablespoons single cream	$\frac{1}{3}$ cup coffee cream

Peel the potatoes and cut into medium-sized pieces. Cook in the stock with the seasoning until soft. Meanwhile wash the lettuce and remove the thick stems. Tear the leaves into pieces and add to the potatoes with the milk and chervil. Cook for 10 minutes, simmering gently. Add the butter and allow to cool slightly before liquidising. Pour a

little cream on top of the soup before serving.
❀ This soup freezes well but the colour darkens when it is reheated; however the flavour is excellent.
Serves 6

Variation

Watercress soup Substitute watercress for lettuce and garnish with fresh sprigs of watercress before serving.

SMOKED FISH SOUP

IMPERIAL	AMERICAN
1 lb. smoked haddock fillets	1 lb. smoked haddock fillets
2 onions	2 onions
2 potatoes	2 potatoes
1 pint water	$2\frac{1}{2}$ cups water
1 oz. butter	2 tablespoons butter
$\frac{1}{2}$ pint milk	$1\frac{1}{4}$ cups milk
salt and pepper	salt and pepper

Remove the skin from the haddock fillets, place in a pan with the roughly chopped onions and potatoes, cover with the water, and bring to the boil. Simmer gently until the vegetables are cooked; allow to cool slightly and put into the blender. Turn on at medium speed and liquidise until smooth. Heat the butter and milk in a saucepan, return the fish mixture to the milk. Season well and sprinkle with grated parsley.
Serves 6

BORSCHT

IMPERIAL	AMERICAN
8 oz. cooked beetroot	$1\frac{1}{3}$ cups diced cooked beets
$\frac{1}{2}$ lemon	$\frac{1}{2}$ lemon
salt and pepper	salt and pepper
1 small onion	1 small onion
1 pint sour cream	$2\frac{1}{2}$ cups sour cream
to garnish:	**to garnish:**
beetroot diced very small	beet diced very small

Put all the ingredients into the blender including the flesh of the lemon and a small strip of the peel; discard the white pith. Blend on maximum speed until smooth, serve chilled and garnished with diced cooked beetroot.
Serves 4

Dressings and sauces

 **FRENCH DRESSING**
Illustrated on page 19

IMPERIAL	AMERICAN
½ pint oil	1¼ cups oil
5 tablespoons wine vinegar	⅓ cup wine vinegar
¼ teaspoon French mustard	¼ teaspoon French mustard
pinch sugar	pinch sugar
salt and pepper	salt and pepper

Put all the ingredients into the blender and run for about 20 seconds at medium speed. Store in an airtight jar or bottle and shake up before using.

Variations

Garlic dressing Add 1 clove of garlic and 1 slice of lemon.
Herb dressing Add mixed herbs.
Parsley dressing Add 4 sprigs of parsley.

 THOUSAND ISLAND DRESSING

IMPERIAL	AMERICAN
½ pint mayonnaise (see page 17)	1¼ cups mayonnaise (see page 17)
2 tablespoons tomato ketchup	3 tablespoons tomato ketchup
½ small onion	½ small onion
1 stalk celery	1 stalk celery
3 sprigs parsley	3 sprigs parsley
¼ green pepper	¼ green sweet pepper
1 slice canned red pimiento	1 slice canned red pimiento
1 hard-boiled egg	1 hard-cooked egg

All ingredients except the hard-boiled egg should be blended at medium speed until the vegetables are chopped. Shell and quarter the egg and add it to the mixture. Blend until the egg is chopped. Serve with salads, steaks, hamburgers, and fish.

 **AVOCADO MAYONNAISE**

IMPERIAL	AMERICAN
½ avocado pear	½ avocado
juice of ½ lemon	juice of ½ lemon
6 tablespoons oil	½ cup oil
salt and pepper	salt and pepper
½ teaspoon sugar	½ teaspoon sugar

Peel and roughly slice the avocado and place in the blender. Add the lemon juice and blend until smooth. Very gradually add the oil. Finally add the sugar and season to taste. Serve with tomatoes or eggs.

 AIOLI

In order to make this successfully in the blender you must change the method for this famous sauce, which is so popular round the shores of the Mediterranean.

IMPERIAL	AMERICAN
2 cloves garlic	2 cloves garlic
¼ teaspoon salt	¼ teaspoon salt
1 egg	1 egg
½ teaspoon water	½ teaspoon water
½ pint olive oil	1¼ cups olive oil
1 teaspoon lemon juice	1 teaspoon lemon juice

Put the peeled crushed garlic with the salt into the blender, add the egg, and switch on at high speed for several seconds. When the garlic is pulverised run the machine on low speed and pour in the oil in a thin stream. When the mixture thickens increase the speed slightly and add the remaining oil at a slightly faster rate. This sauce is meant to be very thick. Add the lemon juice very carefully when the sauce is removed from the blender. If it is added while the blender is running it may curdle. Serve with raw vegetables; it is also delicious with poached fish.

Variation

This can be made without egg by blending quarter of the oil with the garlic first.

MAYONNAISE

IMPERIAL	AMERICAN
1 whole egg	1 whole egg
salt and pepper	salt and pepper
¼ teaspoon French mustard	¼ teaspoon French mustard
2 tablespoons wine vinegar or lemon juice	3 tablespoons wine vinegar or lemon juice
½ pint vegetable oil, preferably olive	1¼ cups vegetable oil, preferably olive

For blender mayonnaise use the whole egg. Make sure all ingredients are at room temperature, i.e., do not use an egg which has just come out of the refrigerator. Put the egg in the goblet with salt, pepper, mustard, and 1 tablespoon vinegar, cover, and run on minimum speed. Pour in half of the oil very slowly while the machine is running. Stop the motor and add the remaining vinegar or lemon juice, then switch on to maximum speed and pour in the remainder of the oil.

Note: Mayonnaise can separate or curdle if the ingredients are not at room temperature or if the oil is added too quickly. However, all is not lost if this happens–simply begin again:
1. Pour the curdled mixture into a measuring jug.
2. Wash and dry the goblet thoroughly.
3. Break another egg into the blender, turn it on at minimum speed, and add the separated mixture slowly until the blades are well covered.
4. Now turn the machine up to maximum speed and add the remaining ingredients slowly. You may need a little extra oil.

Variations

Garlic mayonnaise Add 1 small clove of garlic.
Herb mayonnaise Add parsley, chives, or chervil.
Mixer mayonnaise Alternatively mayonnaise may be made with a hand mixer, using the sauce ingredients but only the *yolk* of the egg. Put the yolk of the egg into a small bowl with salt, pepper, and mustard. Turn the mixer to minimum speed and drop the oil in slowly. Add vinegar or lemon juice to taste at the end when a thick emulsion is obtained. Should the sauce curdle, start again with a completely clean dry bowl and beaters and another egg yolk. When an emulsion is formed with the egg and a little oil, add the curdled mixture as if you were adding the remaining oil.

1. Use ingredients at room temperature (that means taking the eggs out of the fridge in time!). Remember to use the whole egg when using the blender. Put all the ingredients with the exception of the oil in the blender. Take out the centre cap, switch the speed to 1.

2. Pour in the oil in a thin stream; shield the hole with your hand to avoid splashes until the knives are covered by the mixture. Continue pouring until the desired consistency is reached.

3. Here is an ideal first course of coronets of salami, egg mayonnaise, sardines, tomato vinaigrette, black and green olives, and green pepper salad. This type of food is also ideal for summer picnics with French bread and butter.

COOKED SALAD DRESSING

IMPERIAL	AMERICAN
2 eggs	2 eggs
2 egg yolks	2 egg yolks
2 teaspoons flour	2 teaspoons flour
4 teaspoons sugar	4 teaspoons sugar
mustard	mustard
salt and pepper	salt and pepper
½ pint milk	1¼ cups milk
1 teaspoon butter	1 teaspoon butter
4 tablespoons vinegar	⅓ cup vinegar

Put the eggs, yolks, flour, sugar, mustard, salt, and pepper into a heavy saucepan large enough for the hand mixer to operate in. Beat on maximum speed until smooth. Put the saucepan on a low heat, reduce speed to medium, gradually add milk, and finally add the butter. Raise the heat and beat well, cooking until thick. Add the vinegar, remove from the heat and allow to cool. This sauce keeps in the refrigerator for a longer time than ordinary mayonnaise.

WHITE SAUCE

IMPERIAL	AMERICAN
1 pint milk	2½ cups milk
2 oz. butter	¼ cup butter
2 oz. flour	½ cup all-purpose flour
salt and pepper	salt and pepper

Heat the milk and butter, then pour half into the blender. Add the flour and seasoning, switch on to maximum for a few seconds, then return to the saucepan with the other half of the milk. Cook over a low heat until thick.

Variations

Cheese sauce Add 4 oz. (U.S. 1 cup) grated cheese, a dash of mustard, and a pinch of cayenne pepper and blend with the basic sauce.
Mushroom sauce Add 4 oz. (U.S. 1 cup) mushrooms which have been sautéed in butter or blanched in boiling water.
Béchamel sauce Heat the milk slowly with an onion, a few peppercorns, and a pinch of nutmeg. Strain the milk into the blender and make as basic sauce.

HOLLANDAISE SAUCE

IMPERIAL	AMERICAN
8 oz. butter	1 cup butter
1 tablespoon water	1 tablespoon water
1 teaspoon vinegar	1 teaspoon vinegar
4 egg yolks	4 egg yolks
2 tablespoons lemon juice	3 tablespoons lemon juice
salt	salt
freshly milled pepper	freshly milled pepper

Melt the butter with the water and vinegar in a saucepan–*do not allow it to brown*. Put the egg yolks, lemon juice, and seasoning into the goblet and turn on at minimum speed. Now pour the melted butter into the goblet in a steady stream; the sauce should now be fairly thick. Serve immediately if possible. Alternatively, keep warm over a pan of warm water but stir continually as it tends to thicken at the bottom. Should you forget and allow the sauce to become thick return it to the blender and add a few drops of warm water and a few drops of lemon juice. Blend until smooth again.

This sauce is delicious with fish and vegetables, especially asparagus.

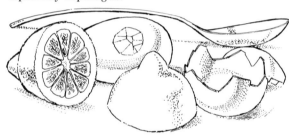

BEARNAISE SAUCE

IMPERIAL	AMERICAN
1 small onion or shallot	1 small onion or shallot
3 tablespoons white wine	¼ cup white wine
2 teaspoons tarragon vinegar	2 teaspoons tarragon vinegar
1 teaspoon fresh or ½ teaspoon dried tarragon	1 teaspoon fresh or ½ teaspoon dried tarragon
freshly milled black pepper	freshly milled black pepper
few drops lemon juice	few drops lemon juice
½ pint hollandaise sauce (see above)	1¼ cups hollandaise sauce (see above)

Put the onion, finely chopped, in a saucepan with the wine, vinegar, tarragon, pepper, and lemon juice and allow to boil until the liquid is reduced to a few drops. Blend the mixture with the hollandaise sauce for a few seconds at maximum speed. This is delicious with chicken and meat.

Macaroni twist salad (page 33) with French dressing (page 16)

BARBECUE SAUCE

IMPERIAL	AMERICAN
1 large onion	1 large onion
$\frac{1}{2}$ green pepper	$\frac{1}{2}$ green sweet pepper
1 chilli pepper	1 chili pepper
1 teaspoon mustard	1 teaspoon mustard
2 tablespoons vinegar	3 tablespoons vinegar
salt	salt
few drops Tabasco sauce	few drops Tabasco sauce
1 tablespoon Worcestershire sauce	1 tablespoon Worcestershire sauce
4 tablespoons oil	$\frac{1}{3}$ cup oil
4 tablespoons red wine (optional)	$\frac{1}{3}$ cup red wine (optional)

Chop the vegetables roughly and put all the ingredients except half of the wine in the blender until the vegetables are finely chopped. Use for basting chicken and pork. Serve the remainder heated with the remaining red wine as a sauce.

CREOLE SAUCE

IMPERIAL	AMERICAN
2 tablespoons oil	3 tablespoons oil
1 large onion	1 large onion
1 clove garlic	1 clove garlic
1 green pepper	1 green sweet pepper
1 chilli pepper (optional)	1 chili pepper (optional)
1 stalk celery	1 stalk celery
2 tablespoons vinegar	3 tablespoons vinegar
7-oz. can tomatoes	7-oz. can tomatoes
1 teaspoon sugar	1 teaspoon sugar
$\frac{1}{4}$ teaspoon oregano	$\frac{1}{4}$ teaspoon oregano

Heat the oil in a saucepan, add the roughly chopped onion, garlic, peppers, and celery, and allow to sauté gently for at least 5 minutes. Place the vegetables in the goblet and switch on at medium speed until the vegetables are finely chopped. Add the remaining ingredients and blend all together. Return to the saucepan and simmer for at least 10 to 15 minutes. Serve with shrimps, prawns, minced beef, or diced cooked meat, with rice or pasta, for an excellent savoury meal.

CURRY SAUCE

IMPERIAL	AMERICAN
1 oz. butter	2 tablespoons butter
1 tablespoon oil	1 tablespoon oil
1 carrot	1 carrot
1 clove garlic	1 clove garlic
1 small potato	1 small potato
2 teaspoons curry powder	2 teaspoons curry powder
1 teaspoon tomato purée	1 teaspoon tomato paste
salt	salt
few drops lemon juice	few drops lemon juice
$\frac{1}{2}$ pint stock	$1\frac{1}{4}$ cups stock

Melt the butter in a saucepan, add the oil, and sauté the roughly chopped vegetables for about 5 minutes, stirring all the time. Turn up the heat and sprinkle the vegetables with curry powder; stir around the saucepan for a few seconds. Place the vegetables in the goblet and switch on at medium speed until they are liquidised. Add the tomato purée, seasoning, lemon juice, and some of the stock; switch on again for a few seconds. Return to the saucepan with the remaining stock and simmer for at least 10 minutes. Serve with fish, meat, or vegetables on a bed of rice.

TARTARE SAUCE

IMPERIAL	AMERICAN
8 gherkins	4 dill pickles
3 tablespoons capers	$\frac{1}{4}$ cup capers
8 tablespoons mayonnaise (see page 17)	$\frac{2}{3}$ cup mayonnaise (see page 17)
$\frac{1}{2}$ teaspoon lemon juice	$\frac{1}{2}$ teaspoon lemon juice

Chop the gherkins and capers by putting them in the blender, switched on at maximum speed, for a few seconds. Add remaining ingredients and blend well. Serve with fried fish.

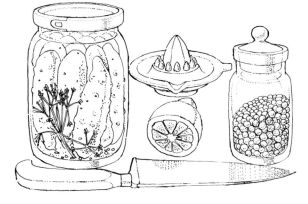

CUCUMBER SAUCE

IMPERIAL	AMERICAN
4 tablespoons sour cream	⅓ cup sour cream
4 tablespoons mayonnaise (see page 17)	⅓ cup mayonnaise (see page 17)
½ cucumber	½ cucumber
½ teaspoon salt	½ teaspoon salt
1½ tablespoons lemon juice	2 tablespoons lemon juice

Mix the sour cream and the mayonnaise in a bowl. Place the other ingredients in the blender, having cut the cucumber roughly. Cover the blender and switch on until the cucumber is smooth. Add the blended cucumber gradually to the mixture in the bowl. Serve with cold fish.

TOMATO SAUCE

IMPERIAL	AMERICAN
1 medium onion	1 medium onion
4 oz. mushrooms (optional)	1 cup sliced mushrooms (optional)
1 can peeled tomatoes or 1 lb. fresh tomatoes	1 can peeled tomatoes or 1 lb. fresh tomatoes
1 clove garlic	1 clove garlic
salt and pepper	salt and pepper
1 teaspoon sugar	1 teaspoon sugar
½ teaspoon oregano	½ teaspoon oregano
3 tablespoons tomato purée	¼ cup tomato paste
¼ pint red wine or stock	⅔ cup red wine or stock

Roughly chop the onion and mushrooms. Peel the tomatoes if using fresh and cut into two or three pieces. Put all the ingredients into the blender at high speed until smooth; you may have to liquidise in batches depending on the size of your machine. Simmer in a covered saucepan for 25 minutes. Use with fish, meat, pasta, or rice.

PLUM SAUCE

IMPERIAL	AMERICAN
4 oz. plum jam	⅓ cup plum jam
¼ teaspoon mixed herbs	¼ teaspoon mixed herbs
2 tablespoons vinegar	3 tablespoons vinegar
pinch allspice	pinch allspice
2 teaspoons dry mustard	2 teaspoons dry mustard

Place all the ingredients in the blender and switch on at medium speed until everything is well blended. This sauce is delicious with roast pork, pork chops, or duck.

ORANGE AND CRANBERRY SAUCE

IMPERIAL	AMERICAN
1 orange	1 orange
3 tablespoons water	¼ cup water
4 oz. sugar	½ cup sugar
8 oz. cranberries	2 cups cranberries

Cut the orange into about eight pieces, remove the pips, then put the sections into the blender. Add the water and sugar, cover the goblet, and switch on at a medium speed for about 10 seconds until the orange peel is coarsely cut. Add the cranberries and blend until the whole fruit begins to disappear. Do not completely pulverise the fruit. Serve raw, or simmer for 15 minutes. Chill before serving with roast poultry.

APPLE SAUCE

IMPERIAL	AMERICAN
2 large cooking apples	2 large cooking apples
3 tablespoons water	¼ cup water
2 teaspoons lemon juice	2 teaspoons lemon juice
1½ oz. sugar	3 tablespoons sugar
knob of butter	knob of butter

Wash, peel, and core the apples and cut into 1-inch cubes. Put half the apple cubes with the water, lemon juice, and sugar into the blender and run on minimum speed until the apples are liquidised. Turn to high speed and add the remaining apples gradually. Melt the butter in a saucepan and add the apple sauce, cook for a few minutes, and then serve. ❋ This sauce can be kept in the freezer in small plastic jars.

MINT SAUCE

IMPERIAL	AMERICAN
fresh mint leaves	fresh mint leaves
2 teaspoons sugar	2 teaspoons sugar
1 tablespoon boiling water	1 tablespoon boiling water
2 tablespoons vinegar	3 tablespoons vinegar

Place all the ingredients in the blender and allow to run until the mint leaves are chopped into fairly small pieces. Allow to stand for at least half an hour before serving.

HORSERADISH SAUCE

IMPERIAL	AMERICAN
2 tablespoons horseradish or 4 tablespoons finely grated bottled horseradish	3 tablespoons horseradish or $\frac{1}{3}$ cup finely grated bottled horseradish
$\frac{1}{2}$ pint béchamel sauce (see page 18)	$1\frac{1}{4}$ cups béchamel sauce (see page 18)
1 teaspoon wine vinegar	1 teaspoon wine vinegar
2 tablespoons cream	3 tablespoons cream

Chop the horseradish in the blender, add the other ingredients, and blend thoroughly. Heat through and serve with roast beef.

ORANGE BRANDY BUTTER

IMPERIAL	AMERICAN
2 oz. butter	$\frac{1}{4}$ cup butter
2 oz. castor sugar	$\frac{1}{4}$ cup sugar
2 oz. icing sugar	$\frac{1}{2}$ cup sifted confectioners' sugar
2 tablespoons brandy	3 tablespoons brandy
rind of $\frac{1}{4}$ orange	rind of $\frac{1}{4}$ orange

Cream the butter and sugars together with the mixer until the mixture is pale and fluffy as in the first creaming stage of making a cake. Gradually add the brandy and finally the grated orange rind, mixing well. Pipe or pile into a dish and keep in a cool place until needed.

This hard sauce is delicious with Christmas pudding and mince pies. The orange rind can be omitted; or a mixture of lemon and orange rind is excellent served with a plain steamed pudding. As this sauce is rich very little is needed. ❄ If there is any left over it will keep well in the freezer.

RUM BUTTER

IMPERIAL	AMERICAN
4 oz. butter	$\frac{1}{2}$ cup butter
8 oz. soft brown sugar	1 cup brown sugar, firmly packed
$\frac{1}{4}$ teaspoon cinnamon	$\frac{1}{4}$ teaspoon cinnamon
1–2 tablespoons rum	1–2 tablespoons rum

Cream the butter, sugar, and cinnamon together with the mixer until soft. Gradually add the rum and mix until the sugar and butter are well creamed. Store in small pots and serve with steamed fruit or sponge puddings. This butter sauce is also very good with mince pies.

CHOCOLATE SAUCE

IMPERIAL	AMERICAN
2 oz. plain chocolate	$\frac{1}{3}$ cup semi-sweet chocolate pieces
2 oz. sugar	$\frac{1}{4}$ cup sugar
$\frac{1}{4}$ pint water	$\frac{2}{3}$ cup water
1 teaspoon brandy or rum	1 teaspoon brandy or rum
2 tablespoons cream	3 tablespoons cream

Break the chocolate into pieces and chop finely in the blender. Dissolve the sugar in the water and bring to the boil, add the chocolate and stir into the syrup. Add the brandy or rum and the cream just before serving. This sauce is delicious served hot or cold with chocolate sponge pudding (see page 49) or ice cream.

CUSTARD SAUCE

IMPERIAL	AMERICAN
1 egg	1 egg
2 teaspoons castor sugar	2 teaspoons castor sugar
$\frac{1}{2}$ teaspoon vanilla essence	$\frac{1}{2}$ teaspoon vanilla extract
8 tablespoons milk	$\frac{2}{3}$ cup milk

Put the egg in the blender with the sugar and essence. Switch on to beat the egg. Bring the milk almost to boiling point. Strain into the blender, switch on for a few seconds. Return to the saucepan and cook very gently until the custard thickens. If any lumps appear through the sauce put back into the blender until smooth.

LEMON SAUCE

IMPERIAL	AMERICAN
2 lemons	2 lemons
7–8 tablespoons water	$\frac{1}{2}$–$\frac{2}{3}$ cup water
2–3 tablespoons sugar	3–4 tablespoons sugar

Peel a thin rind from the lemons, put into the blender to chop finely. Put the water in a saucepan with the sugar. Squeeze the lemons and add 1 tablespoon strained juice to the sugar and water. Add the lemon rind and simmer until a thick syrup is obtained.

Variation

Substitute 2 oranges for the lemons to make orange sauce.

Kipper cakes (page 25)

Fish

Fish can add so much variety to the menu that it seems a pity it is so often ignored. I think one of the reasons for this is that, for children, fish is something of an acquired taste and many mothers become tired of trying to persuade them to eat it. It is well worth persevering because fish can so often provide the answer when you are looking for variety, and some of the cheapest fish are the most nutritious.

In addition to the fish starters, dips, and sandwich fillings which can be made with the mixer and blender and are to be found in other sections, I have included the preparation of simple fish dishes, some of which can be served with a sauce from the sauce section.

With the blender, fresh or toasted breadcrumbs are readily available for coating fish, so much nicer than packaged crumbs.

Buying fresh fish

There is nothing more off-putting than fish which is not fresh. Modern methods of packing and transporting fish are excellent but sometimes we see some very tired fish in the shops. Avoid buying this as it only turns the family against what can be a most excellent meal.
1. A fish which has dull eyes and limp flesh is not fresh. The eyes should be brilliant and the flesh stiff.
2. The smell will be unpleasant when the flesh is really limp.
3. A finger mark on a fresh fish will disappear quickly; on a less fresh one it will linger.

FRIED FISH

IMPERIAL	AMERICAN
4 fillets white fish	4 fillets white fish
to coat:	**to coat:**
salt and pepper	salt and pepper
1 egg	1 egg
3 oz. fresh white breadcrumbs	1½ cups fresh white bread crumbs
cooking oil	cooking oil

Pat the fish fillets dry with a clean piece of kitchen paper, dip in the seasoned beaten egg, then dip in the crumbs. Pat crumbs into the fish firmly then dip back into the egg and again into the crumbs. This double coating gives an excellent finish to the fish. Pat the crumbs firmly onto the surface before frying. Use oil to fry the fish; there should be enough to cover the pieces of fish completely. It is advisable to store this oil separately and use again only for fish.

Allow the oil to become really hot. Test with a cube of bread if you are unsure. Put the cube into the fat and it should brown and come to the surface very quickly. Remember the fat will cool down quickly when the fish is added, so do not put too many pieces into the pan at once or the fish will be soggy. Fry until golden brown. Serve when crisp, garnished with lemon and parsley, and accompanied by tartare or tomato sauce (see pages 20 and 21).
Serves 4

CRISPY PLAICE CURLS

IMPERIAL	AMERICAN
8 oz. long-grain rice	generous cup long-grain rice
1½ lb. plaice fillets	1½ lb. plaice or flounder fillets
2 oz. flour	½ cup all-purpose flour
salt and pepper	salt and pepper
2 eggs	2 eggs
6 oz. fresh white breadcrumbs	3 cups fresh white bread crumbs
cooking oil	cooking oil
to garnish:	**to garnish:**
4 sprigs watercress	4 sprigs watercress
4 lemon wedges	4 lemon wedges

Cook the rice in boiling salted water (2 cups water to 1 cup rice) until the water is absorbed and the rice is dry and separate. Keep warm until the fish is cooked.

Skin the fillets or ask the fishmonger to do this when he is filleting the fish. Cut the fillets into strips. Dip the strips into the seasoned flour, shake the surplus flour away, then dip in beaten egg and breadcrumbs. Fry the strips in hot oil until crisp and golden brown. Drain well on soft kitchen paper.

Serve the fish on a bed of rice garnished with watercress and wedges of lemon. Accompany by tomato, tartare, or béarnaise sauce (see pages 18, 20, and 21).
Serves 4

SEA FOOD CREOLE

IMPERIAL	AMERICAN
6 oz. peeled prawns	1 cup peeled prawns or shrimp
4 scallops	4 scallops
creole sauce (see page 20)	creole sauce (see page 20)
salt and pepper	salt and pepper
8 oz. long-grain rice	generous cup long-grain rice
slice of lemon	slice of lemon
to garnish:	**to garnish:**
lemon wedges	lemon wedges
parsley	parsley

Add the prawns and chopped scallops to the creole sauce and allow to simmer gently for at least 10 minutes. Season to taste. Meanwhile cook the rice using 1 cup rice to 2 cups boiling salted water. Add the slice of lemon to the rice while it is cooking as it adds flavour and keeps the rice white. Serve the rice in a heated serving dish, arrange the seafood down the centre of the dish, and garnish with lemon wedges and parsley sprigs.
Serves 4

KIPPER CAKES
Illustrated on page 23

IMPERIAL	AMERICAN
1 lb. potatoes, peeled and boiled in salted water	1 lb. potatoes, peeled and boiled in salted water
3 tablespoons cream	$\frac{1}{4}$ cup cream
1 oz. butter	2 tablespoons butter
2 7-oz. cans kipper fillets, drained, or 1 lb. kipper fillets	2 7-oz. cans kipper fillets, drained, or 1 lb. kipper fillets
2 tablespoons chopped parsley	3 tablespoons chopped parsley
salt	salt
freshly ground black pepper	freshly ground black pepper
dash Tabasco sauce	dash Tabasco sauce
2 tablespoons lemon juice	3 tablespoons lemon juice
1 egg	1 egg
to coat:	**to coat:**
flour	all-purpose flour
1 egg, beaten	1 egg, beaten
dried breadcrumbs	dry bread crumbs

Cream the potatoes in the mixer with the cream and butter until smooth. Blend the kipper fillets until very smooth and add to the potato with the parsley, seasoning, Tabasco sauce, and lemon juice. If using fresh kipper fillets remove the skins before blending. Beat well, then bind together with the egg. Form into croquette shapes. Flour, then dip in egg and breadcrumbs. Fry in deep fat until golden brown and crisp. Drain on kitchen paper and serve hot.
Serves 4

Variations

Salmon cakes Substitute 8 to 12 oz. fresh or canned salmon. Salmon cakes made with the remains of a whole salmon make a most delicious breakfast dish.

Fish cakes Substitute 12 oz. cod or haddock which has been poached in $\frac{1}{4}$ pint (U.S. $\frac{2}{3}$ cup) milk. No cream is necessary. However, use the liquid in which the fish has been poached. Serve as a supper dish with tomato sauce (see page 21).

SALMON LOAF

IMPERIAL	AMERICAN
3 oz. fresh breadcrumbs	1$\frac{1}{2}$ cups fresh bread crumbs
8-oz. can salmon	8-oz. can salmon
2 eggs	2 eggs
1 oz. butter	2 tablespoons butter
1 slice onion	1 slice onion
$\frac{1}{2}$ teaspoon celery salt	$\frac{1}{2}$ teaspoon celery salt
2 sprigs parsley	2 sprigs parsley
pinch dry mustard	pinch dry mustard
pepper	pepper
$\frac{1}{4}$ pint milk	$\frac{2}{3}$ cup milk

Make the breadcrumbs in the usual way by pushing a few pieces of bread at a time into the goblet while the blender is running. Empty the crumbs out into a bowl. Put the remainder of the ingredients into the goblet and switch on at medium speed until everything is blended well. Pour the mixture into the crumbs and mix well. Bake in a greased 1-lb. loaf tin in a moderately hot oven for about 45 minutes until golden brown. Serve hot with a sauce or cold with salad and cucumber sauce (see page 21).
Serves 4
Cooking time 45 minutes
Temperature 375°F., 190°C., Gas Mark 5

GRILLED SALMON

IMPERIAL	AMERICAN
4 salmon steaks	4 salmon steaks
4 oz. butter	$\frac{1}{2}$ cup butter
freshly milled black pepper	freshly milled black pepper
hollandaise sauce (see page 18)	hollandaise sauce (see page 18)
to garnish:	**to garnish:**
4 tomatoes	4 tomatoes
4-oz. packet frozen spinach	4-oz. package frozen spinach
4 slices lemon	4 slices lemon

Arrange the salmon steaks on the grill pan, score the flesh with a knife, and spread softened butter over each steak. Sprinkle with pepper. Make the hollandaise sauce. Halve the tomatoes and remove the insides (these can be used in a sandwich filling). Heat the frozen spinach, add a little cream after the spinach is drained if you feel extravagant. Mix the spinach with 2 tablespoons of the hollandaise sauce in the blender and stuff into the halved tomatoes. Pop into a moderate oven (350°F., 180°C., Gas Mark 4) for 10 to 15 minutes. Now grill the salmon starting off under a hot grill and reducing after a few minutes to allow heat to penetrate the thickness of the slice. Turn over and baste with melted butter. Return to the grill to allow the underside to be cooked. Serve on a heated dish garnished with lemon wedges and stuffed tomatoes. Sauté or boiled new potatoes make an excellent accompaniment. Serve the remaining hollandaise sauce in a sauceboat.
Serves 4

FISH MOUSSE
Illustrated on the cover

IMPERIAL	AMERICAN
8 oz. boned white fish	$\frac{1}{2}$ lb. boned white fish
$\frac{1}{2}$ oz. gelatine	2 envelopes gelatin
1 teaspoon tomato purée	1 teaspoon tomato paste
salt and pepper	salt and pepper
$\frac{1}{4}$ pint double cream	$\frac{2}{3}$ cup whipping cream
4 egg yolks	4 egg yolks
2 egg whites	2 egg whites
to decorate:	**to decorate:**
slices of lemon or apple	slices of lemon or apple
parsley	parsley

Steam the fish until cooked, melt the gelatine with a little fish liquid, allow to cool. Grease a 7-inch soufflé dish. Tie a greased strip of greaseproof paper round the top. Blend the fish with the gelatine, tomato purée, and seasoning until smooth. Half whip the cream and add to the blended mixture. Whisk the egg yolks until thick, light, and fluffy.

Fold the fish mixture into the egg yolk mixture. Lastly whisk the egg whites with the mixer until white and stiff. Fold into the fish mixture and pour into the soufflé dish. Allow to set in the refrigerator before removing the paper. Decorate round the edge with chopped parsley. Slices of tomato, cucumber, apple, or lemon can be used to decorate the top.
Serves 6

FISH PIE

IMPERIAL	AMERICAN
1$\frac{1}{2}$ lb. filleted white fish	1$\frac{1}{2}$ lb. filleted white fish
1 pint béchamel sauce (see page 18)	2$\frac{1}{2}$ cups béchamel sauce (see page 18)
salt and pepper	salt and pepper
2 tablespoons cream	3 tablespoons cream
$\frac{1}{2}$ teaspoon tarragon	$\frac{1}{2}$ teaspoon tarragon
2 hard-boiled eggs	2 hard-cooked eggs
8 oz. tomatoes	$\frac{1}{2}$ lb. tomatoes
8 oz. puff pastry or 8 oz. blender pastry (see page 66)	$\frac{1}{2}$ lb. frozen puff paste or $\frac{1}{2}$ lb. blender pastry (see page 66)

Cook the filleted fish (haddock or cod) for about 10 minutes in some of the milk to be used for the sauce. Make up the sauce and add the fish liquid and seasoning. Stir the cream into the sauce. Flake the fish in the bottom of a pie dish, season well, and sprinkle with a little tarragon. Pour over a quarter of the sauce. Chop the hard-boiled eggs and sprinkle on top of the fish; add a little more sauce. Dip the tomatoes in boiling water and remove the skins. Slice the tomatoes and place in a layer over the hard-boiled egg; season well and cover with the remaining sauce. Roll out the pastry, place on top of the pie dish, and pinch the edges to make an attractive edge (see rolling out pastry page 65). Brush over with beaten egg and cook in a hot oven until golden brown.
Serves 6
Cooking time about 20 minutes
Temperature 450°F., 230°C., Gas Mark 8

Variation

Cheesy fish pie Add a further layer by sprinkling grated cheese over the sauce. Substitute mashed potatoes for the pastry. Cook 3 lb. potatoes in boiling salted water until soft, drain, and then add 2 oz. (U.S. $\frac{1}{4}$ cup) butter and seasoning. Beat thoroughly with the mixer then add 1 egg and 2 oz. (U.S. $\frac{1}{2}$ cup) grated cheese. Beat until smooth and for a glamorous finish pipe on top of the fish or spread over and mark in a pattern with a fork. Sprinkle the potatoes with grated cheese and dot with butter. Cook as directed above.

Fruited duck (page 40) and pineapple water-lily pudding (page 52)

Meat

The mixer and blender make light work of meat dishes that need a lot of chopping and mixing. Stuffings can be made in the wink of an eye, allowing attractive dishes to be made easily with the more economical cuts of meat. Use the mincing attachment, if you have one, to help with the leftovers. In the blender you can make marinades which will tenderise and flavour the meat. Sauces can be made easily, giving new and exciting variety to your main meal of the day.

Use the following recipes as a guide, then start experimenting yourself.

Roasting meat

When cooking meat dishes it is always better to preheat the oven. The chart below gives suggested temperatures and cooking times for roasting, together with some accompaniments which go well with each type of meat. The thermometer readings in brackets are what the meat thermometer will read when the joint is done.

❋ All roasts can be cooked directly from the freezer but the cooking time must be extended to allow the meat to cook right through.

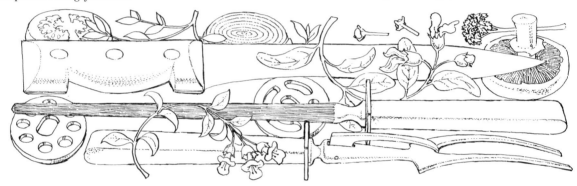

TO ROAST	TEMPERATURE	TIME	ACCOMPANIMENTS
	Put all meat into a hot oven for 10-15 minutes– 450°F., 230°C., Gas Mark 8.		
BEEF	Reduce to 350°F., 180°C., Gas Mark 4 (thermometer reading 140°F. rare, 160°F. medium).	15 minutes per lb. and 15 minutes over	Yorkshire pudding (see page 29) Horseradish sauce (see page 22) Thin gravy
LAMB	Reduce to 325°F., 170°C., Gas Mark 3 (thermometer reading 170°F.).	25 minutes per lb. and 25 minutes over	Mint sauce (see page 21) Medium thick gravy
PORK	Reduce to 350°F., 180°C., Gas Mark 4 (thermometer reading 185°F.).	30 minutes per lb. and 30 minutes over	Sage and onion stuffing (see page 29) Apple sauce (see page 21) Thickened gravy
VEAL	Reduce to 325°F., 170°C., Gas Mark 3 (thermometer reading 175°F.).	30 minutes per lb. and 30 minutes over	Veal forcemeat (see page 32) Bacon rolls Thickened gravy

Roast beef

Cook as directed in the chart. There are several schools of thought on whether meat can be used straight from the freezer or whether it should be thawed out. My own experience with beef is that a well-hung piece of meat will cook well either way but meat which is not well hung will still be a little tough. This is not because it has been frozen, as many people seem to think. (Hardly any beef is allowed to hang long enough these days, as it is uneconomical for the butcher to take up space in his shop.) ❀ I have devised a foolproof method of obtaining delicious roast beef from my freezer; you may like to give it a try. It simply entails leaving the beef in a cool place for 24 to 48 hours, preferably uncovered, either before freezing it or after. This can be inconvenient but I think the result is worth it. A good piece of beef should have dark red flesh and firm yellow fat.

Gravy Pour off the fat from the roasting tin very slowly so that all the sediment and meat juices remain. Season the sediment which remains in the tin and mix well over the heat until it is dark brown. Add about ½ pint (U.S. 1¼ cups) stock (make up with a beef cube) and bring to the boil in the tin, stir well, and boil until a good flavour is obtained. Pour into a gravy boat and skim any fat off before serving.

YORKSHIRE PUDDING

IMPERIAL	AMERICAN
4 oz. plain flour	1 cup all-purpose flour
pinch salt	pinch salt
1 egg	1 egg
½ pint milk	1¼ cups milk

Sieve the flour and salt into the mixer bowl, make a well in the centre, and break the egg into it. Add a little milk and beat with the mixer until a smooth batter is obtained. Gradually stir in the remaining milk with a spoon. To make the batter in the blender place the salt, egg, and milk in the goblet and switch on at minimum speed for 30 seconds. Remove the lid and pour in the sieved flour. Replace the lid and blend for a further 30 seconds. If possible, allow to stand in a cool place for at least 15 minutes before using. Pour the meat fat into individual patty tins or put 3 tablespoons into a shallow ovenproof dish. Allow the fat to heat until very hot and then pour in the batter and bake in a very hot oven for 15 minutes for individual puddings and 30 minutes for a large one.

Serves 4
Cooking time 15–30 minutes depending on size
Temperature 450°F., 230°C., Gas Mark 8

Roast lamb

Cook as directed in the chart. Lamb is particularly delicious when allowed to stand in a marinade as in the recipe for marinated leg of lamb; it can even be frozen in a marinade. Lamb can be cooked straight from the freezer quite successfully but it requires a longer cooking time and it should *not* be put into a hot oven initially.

Gravy Keep about 1 tablespoon fat in the tin with sediment and mix this with 1 tablespoon flour. Blend well and then continue as for beef gravy.

Roast pork

Pork must be well cooked, therefore it is important to know the exact weight of the joint to ensure that it is cooked throughout. ❀ It may be cooked straight from the freezer but allow 1 hour per lb. cooking time. Serve with thickened gravy as lamb.

SAGE AND ONION STUFFING

IMPERIAL	AMERICAN
6 slices white bread	6 slices white bread
4 onions	4 onions
1 egg	1 egg
1 teaspoon sage	1 teaspoon sage
¼ teaspoon thyme	¼ teaspoon thyme
few sprigs parsley	few sprigs parsley
salt and pepper	salt and pepper

Remove the crusts from the bread. Quarter the slices and make into breadcrumbs in the blender. Meanwhile partly boil the roughly chopped onions for a few minutes. Put the breadcrumbs in a bowl, then put the onions into the goblet with the other ingredients and blend until the onion is finely chopped. Mix together with the breadcrumbs and bake in a well-greased tin until the stuffing is firm and golden brown. Put the stuffing in the oven about 25 minutes before the pork is due to be taken out.

CROWN ROAST WITH APRICOTS AND ROSEMARY
Illustrated opposite

IMPERIAL	AMERICAN
14 chops formed into a crown roast	14 chops formed into a crown roast
to stuff:	**to stuff:**
4 oz. fresh breadcrumbs	2 cups fresh bread crumbs
1 onion	1 onion
1 oz. walnuts	$\frac{1}{4}$ cup walnuts
1 egg	1 egg
few sprigs rosemary	few sprigs rosemary
1 lb. dried or 1$\frac{1}{2}$ lb. fresh apricots	1 lb. dried or 1$\frac{1}{2}$ lb. fresh apricots
salt and pepper	salt and pepper
to garnish:	**to garnish:**
1 small can apricot halves or several fresh poached apricots	1 small can apricot halves or several fresh poached apricots
several sprigs rosemary	several sprigs rosemary

Ask the butcher to prepare the chops into a crown. This roast is so popular now that most butchers are willing to do this if you give them a little advance warning. If you can persuade him to mince the scraps of meat which he trims away the mince can be used in the stuffing. Prepare the stuffing by making the fresh white breadcrumbs in the blender. Put into a medium-sized bowl ready for the other ingredients. Cut up the onion roughly and chop in the blender, add the walnuts, switch on for a few seconds, then add the egg and the first lot of rosemary. When this is chopped add to the breadcrumbs in the bowl. Now chop the apricots roughly in the blender and add to the other ingredients with seasoning. Add mince if desired. This mixture should give a moist stuffing. If using dried apricots be sure to steep them in water for several hours before using them.

Now stuff the mixture into the centre of the crown, wrap tinfoil over the ends of the chops to avoid charring, and cook in a moderate oven allowing 30 minutes for each pound of meat. About 10 minutes before serving time place the halved apricots on top of the stuffing, brush with melted butter, and return to the oven. Decorate between the chops with a garland of rosemary (see photograph opposite). Cutlet frills can be put onto the ends of the chops when the foil is removed. Serve with roast potatoes and petit pois.
Serves 6
Cooking time 30 minutes per lb.
Temperature 350°F., 180°C., Gas Mark 4

❀ **Note:** The crown can be prepared in advance and frozen with the stuffing.

Variation

Serve the crown roast filled with new vegetables if you do not want to use a stuffing. The apricot stuffing is also delicious in a stuffed breast of lamb.

MARINATED LEG OF LAMB
Illustrated opposite

IMPERIAL	AMERICAN
1 glass red wine	1 glass red wine
2 tablespoons chopped fresh mint	3 tablespoons chopped fresh mint
1 teaspoon dried or a good sized sprig fresh rosemary	1 teaspoon dried or a good sized sprig fresh rosemary
1 teaspoon salt	1 teaspoon salt
1 clove garlic	1 clove garlic
several sprigs parsley	several sprigs parsley
2 onions	2 onions
wedge of lemon	wedge of lemon
3 tablespoons olive oil	$\frac{1}{4}$ cup olive oil
3$\frac{1}{2}$- to 4-lb. leg of lamb	3$\frac{1}{2}$- to 4-lb. leg of lamb

Put the wine, mint, rosemary, salt, garlic, and parsley into the blender and switch on for a few seconds. Cut up the onions roughly and put into the goblet, then peel the rind from the lemon and add the flesh to the mixture (not the pith).

Blend on medium speed then reduce speed and add the oil. Put the leg of lamb into a casserole or a plastic bag, pour on the marinade, and cover or seal the bag. Allow to stand in a cool place or in the refrigerator for 12 to 24 hours. Remove the meat from the marinade but retain the mixture. Roast in a moderate oven for 1 hour. Pour the marinade over the roast and continue cooking for a further half hour. Carve the roast and serve the marinade mixed with the lamb juices in place of gravy. This makes a delicious main course for a special dinner party.
❀ You can freeze the leg of lamb in a plastic bag with the marinade.
Serves 6
Cooking time 1$\frac{1}{2}$ hours
Temperature 350°F., 180°C., Gas Mark 4

Crown roast with apricots and rosemary and marinated leg of lamb

BEEF OLIVES

IMPERIAL	AMERICAN
12 oz. topside of beef	¾ lb. beef bottom round
half quantity veal	half quantity veal
forcemeat (see below)	forcemeat (see below)
2 tablespoons oil	3 tablespoons oil
1 onion	1 onion
1 carrot	1 carrot
1 tablespoon flour	1 tablespoon flour
½ pint beef stock	1¼ cups beef stock
salt and pepper	salt and pepper

Ask the butcher to cut the meat into slices about 3 by 4 inches in size and beat them flat. Otherwise buy the meat in a thick piece. Cut across the grain and flatten with a cutlet bat or wooden rolling pin. Make up the forcemeat and divide it equally amongst the slices of meat. Roll the meat round the stuffing and secure with a skewer or a wooden cocktail stick. Heat the oil in a heavy frying pan and brown the beef olives. Dice the onion and carrot and sauté the vegetables with the meat. Put the beef olives and vegetables in a casserole, sprinkle the flour into the frying pan, and mix with the meat juices. Add the stock and seasoning and mix well for a few minutes, then strain over the olives. Cook for 1½ hours in a covered dish in a moderate oven until the meat is tender. Remove the skewers before serving with mashed potatoes and the vegetables of your choice.
Serves 4
Cooking time 1½ hours
Temperature 350°F., 180°C., Gas Mark 4

VEAL FORCEMEAT

IMPERIAL	AMERICAN
6 slices white bread	6 slices white bread
2 oz. suet	⅓ cup suet
few sprigs parsley	few sprigs parsley
rind of ½ lemon	rind of ½ lemon
salt and pepper	salt and pepper
½ egg	½ egg

Make the bread into crumbs in the blender and empty into a bowl; add the suet. Chop the parsley and lemon rind in the blender, empty onto the breadcrumbs and suet, and add seasoning. Mix together with some of the beaten egg but do not allow the mixture to become too moist. Use for stuffing veal or beef or with poultry.

BEEF FONDUE

A fondue meal is fun as well as being easy on the hostess, but do be very careful with the fondue pot when it is full of hot oil.

IMPERIAL	AMERICAN
1¼ lb. fillet of beef	1¼ lb. beef tenderloin
cooking oil	cooking oil

Cut the beef into small cubes. Heat the oil in the fondue dish and keep it hot over the spirit burner. Each person cooks his or her own meat on the end of a long fork in the hot oil, and eats it with a variety of sauces and relishes. Tomato sauce (see page 21), curry sauce (see page 20), and béarnaise sauce (see page 18) are all excellent. Different mustards should be served, and a large bowl of salad and cheesy baked potatoes (see page 44) are delicious and easy to prepare.
Serves 4

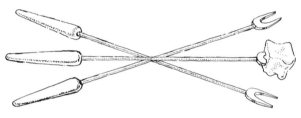

MEAT LOAF

IMPERIAL	AMERICAN
10 water biscuits	3 matzos
1 lb. coarsely minced beef	1 lb. coarsely ground beef
8 oz. coarsely minced pork	½ lb. coarsely ground pork
1 large tomato	1 large tomato
1 small onion	1 small onion
1 small stalk celery	1 small stalk celery
1 small carrot	1 small carrot
2 sprigs parsley	2 sprigs parsley
scant ½ pint milk	1 cup milk
1 egg	1 egg

Crush the water biscuits and make them into crumbs in the blender. Keep the cover on while the machine is running. Empty the crumbs into a bowl. Add the coarsely minced beef and pork to the crumbs. Roughly chop the vegetables. Place the vegetables and remaining ingredients in the goblet and blend until the vegetables are finely chopped. Mix with the meat and crumbs. Put the mixture in a greased 2-lb. loaf tin and bake in a moderate oven for about 1¼ hours. Serve hot or cold.
Serves 8
Cooking time 1¼ hours
Temperature 350°F., 180°C., Gas Mark 4

SAVOURY MEAT LOAF

IMPERIAL	AMERICAN
1 lb. minced beef	1 lb. ground beef
2 oz. fresh white bread-crumbs	1 cup fresh white bread crumbs
1 medium onion	1 medium onion
7-oz. can peeled tomatoes	7-oz. can peeled tomatoes
1 teaspoon tomato purée	1 teaspoon tomato paste
salt and pepper	salt and pepper
few drops Tabasco sauce	few drops Tabasco sauce
1 teaspoon Worcestershire sauce	1 teaspoon Worcestershire sauce
1 egg	1 egg

Preheat the oven to 350°F., 180°C., Gas Mark 4.

Brown the meat in a frying pan then drain off the fat and place the meat in a mixing bowl with the breadcrumbs. Sauté the roughly chopped onion in a little butter or oil; when it is cooled slightly place it in the goblet with the drained tomatoes, tomato purée, seasonings, and egg. Blend until smooth at a medium speed. Add to the meat and breadcrumb mixture and mix well. Put the mixture into a 1-lb. loaf tin and cook in a moderate oven for about 1 hour. Serve with tomato sauce (see page 21). ❄ Meat loaves freeze well but should cut into portions first.
Serves 4–5
Cooking time 1 hour
Temperature 350°F., 180°C., Gas Mark 4

HOLIDAY PIE

IMPERIAL	AMERICAN
1 lb. finely minced lean beef	1 lb. finely ground lean beef
1 onion	1 onion
½ pint stock or water	1¼ cups stock or water
salt and pepper	salt and pepper
1 large can baked beans	1 large can baked beans
1 lb. cooked mashed potatoes	2 cups cooked mashed potato

Brown the beef in a frying pan with a little fat if necessary. Chop the onion finely and add to the meat; add the stock and seasoning when the meat is browned and allow to cook for about 15 minutes. Pour the meat into the bottom of a pie dish or shallow casserole and top with baked beans. Make sure the mashed potatoes are smooth, beat with the mixer with a knob of butter and a little milk until really creamy. Spread over the surface of the beans, mark a design with a fork, dot with butter if you like, and put in a moderate oven for 25 to 30 minutes.
Serves 4
Cooking time 25–30 minutes
Temperature 350°F., 180°C., Gas Mark 4

Variation

Sprinkle the potatoes with 2 oz. (U.S. ½ cup) grated cheese before putting the pie into the oven.

BARBECUED SPARERIBS

IMPERIAL	AMERICAN
2–3 lb. pork spareribs	2–3 lb. pork spareribs
2 quantities barbecue sauce (see page 20)	2 quantities barbecue sauce (see page 20)

Preheat the oven to 450°F., 230°C., Gas Mark 8.

Put the spareribs in a roasting pan in the oven. Allow to cook for about 30 minutes then remove from the oven and brush with the barbecue sauce. Reduce the temperature to 350°F., 180°C., Gas Mark 4 and cook for a further hour, basting the spareribs frequently with the barbecue sauce. It is also advisable to turn the ribs from time to time. Serve the remainder of the sauce warmed with the spareribs. I usually serve a large mixed salad with this dish, and lots of paper napkins!
Serves 4
Cooking time 1½ hours
Temperature 450°F., 230°C., Gas Mark 8, reducing to 350°F., 180°C., Gas Mark 4

MACARONI TWIST SALAD
Illustrated on page 19

IMPERIAL	AMERICAN
8 oz. macaroni twists	½ lb. macaroni twists
1 onion	1 onion
1 green pepper	1 green sweet pepper
1 red pepper	1 red sweet pepper
8 oz. salami	½ lb. salami
12 black and green olives	12 ripe and green olives
¼ pint French dressing (see page 16)	⅔ cup French dressing (see page 16)
salt and pepper	salt and pepper

Cook the macaroni twists until tender. Drain and wash with cold water; allow to cool. Meanwhile chop the onion finely, deseed and dice the green and red pepper, and chop half the salami into small dice. Mix all ingredients together with French dressing, season, and pile into a salad bowl. Serve with sliced salami and a green salad.
Serves 4

SWEET AND SOUR MEAT BALLS

IMPERIAL	AMERICAN
1 lb. minced beef or pork	1 lb. ground beef or pork
seasoning	seasoning
3 green peppers	3 green sweet peppers
3 pineapple rings	3 pineapple rings
sauce:	**sauce:**
1 clove garlic	1 clove garlic
3 teaspoons cornflour	3 teaspoons cornstarch
2 teaspoons soy sauce	2 teaspoons soy sauce
4 tablespoons vinegar	⅓ cup vinegar
2 tablespoons honey	3 tablespoons honey
4 tablespoons chicken	⅓ cup chicken stock
stock	
2 tablespoons sherry	3 tablespoons sherry

Make the seasoned minced beef or pork into small balls. Dip in seasoned flour (optional) and fry in hot oil until cooked and golden brown. Cut the green peppers into strips and boil for 5 minutes, drain. Cut the pineapple slices into 12 pieces. Blend all the sauce ingredients at maximum speed until the garlic is pulverised. Put into a saucepan with the green pepper and pineapple and simmer until thick. Arrange the meat balls in a heated serving dish and pour over the sauce. Serve with 8 oz. cooked drained egg noodles or 8 oz. cooked long-grain rice. It is also possible to buy bean sprouts in many department stores and supermarkets. These can be served as a vegetable by cooking in boiling salted water for about 4 minutes. Reduce heat and allow to simmer, drain when cooked but still crisp. *Serves* 4

SPAGHETTI BOLOGNESE

IMPERIAL	AMERICAN
8 oz. lean minced beef	1 cup lean ground beef
tomato sauce (see page 21)	tomato sauce (see page 21)
8–12 oz. spaghetti	½–¾ lb. spaghetti
½ oz. butter	1 tablespoon butter
grated nutmeg	grated nutmeg
salt and pepper	salt and pepper
Parmesan cheese	Parmesan cheese

Fry the meat until brown then add the tomato sauce and simmer for at least 40 minutes. Cook the spaghetti as directed on the packet. The thickness may vary from brand to brand, but it will usually take around 10 to 12 minutes to be cooked *al dente*, as the Italians say. This means it is still slightly chewy, definitely not soft or mushy. A test for readiness is to bite through a strand and if the central core remains white the pasta needs a little further cooking. Drain the spaghetti into a colander when cooked, melt the butter in the saucepan,

return the spaghetti to the saucepan, and shake well. Sprinkle with grated nutmeg and freshly ground pepper. In Italy the spaghetti and sauce are often combined but this looks rather messy therefore it is better to serve spaghetti with the sauce on top, sprinkled with Parmesan cheese, and allow each person to mix his own together on the plate.
Serves 4

Variation

Spaghetti and seafood sauce Cook the spaghetti as above. Blend 3 peeled tomatoes or a 7-oz. can with 1 peeled onion, 1 clove garlic, oregano, seasoning, and a little water. Simmer for 15 minutes, then add 4 oz. (U.S. ⅔ cup) shrimps. Heat the wine in a frying pan and add 1 pint (U.S. 2½ cups) mussels, scrubbed and with the beards removed. Discard any mussels which will not close when given a sharp tap. When the mussel shells are wide open, sprinkle with chopped parsley. Add the mussel liquid to the tomato sauce. Serve the spaghetti with the sauce and surround the plate with mussels.

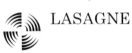

LASAGNE

IMPERIAL	AMERICAN
6 oz. lasagne	⅓ lb. lasagne
1 lb. lean minced beef	1 lb. lean ground beef
tomato sauce (see page 21)	tomato sauce (see page 21)
1 pint béchamel sauce	2½ cups béchamel sauce
(see page 18)	(see page 18)
4 tablespoons cream	⅓ cup cream
salt and pepper	salt and pepper
Parmesan cheese	Parmesan cheese

Cook the lasagne in boiling salted water, with a little oil added to the water, for about 15 minutes. Drain and rinse in cold water. Dry flat on a clean tea-towel. Fry the meat until brown, add the tomato sauce, and simmer for at least 30 minutes. Make up the béchamel sauce and allow to cool slightly before adding the cream. Butter a wide ovenproof dish which is at least 2 inches deep, then put in a layer of meat sauce and a layer of béchamel, as shown in the step-by-step pictures. Now place a layer of lasagne over the sauce and continue to layer until everything is used, ending with a layer of meat sauce topped with béchamel. Coat the surface generously with grated cheese. Cook in a preheated oven for approximately 30 minutes.
Serves 4
Cooking time 30 minutes
Temperature 350°F., 180°C., Gas Mark 4

1. You will need 3 to 4 pints boiling salted water to cook ½ lb. lasagne. I must mention that it is always worth reading the instructions on the pasta pack as some pasta foods are thicker and require longer cooking. I always put a little cooking oil in the water as this prevents any pasta sticking together during cooking.

2. Fold the lasagne into the boiling water gradually to allow it to soften and curl round in the saucepan. Cook for approximately 15 minutes. To test lift a piece out with a fork, allow to cool, then bite. The pasta should be slightly chewy – not mushy but not hard.

3. The meat sauce should be cooked (it may have been made previously). Lay the cooked lasagne on a clean towel to drain and cool. The béchamel sauce should be cooked and ready. I think it is better to put the lasagne together when all the ingredients are cool.

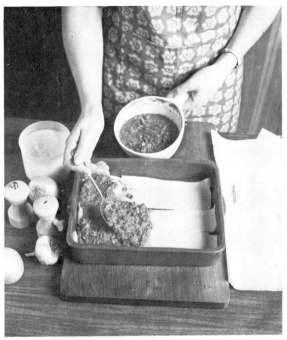

4. Butter a large ovenproof dish and then place layers of pasta and sauces in it. In the picture I have put a layer of lasagne first but you can also start with a layer of meat sauce, followed by a layer of béchamel and finishing with a generous sprinkling of grated cheese, preferably Parmesan.

5. The dish now goes into a preheated moderate oven for about 30 minutes. Do not overcook as the lasagne will become soft and too crisp round the outside of the dish.

Poultry and game

A really delicious roast bird is a dish which any cook can justly serve with pride. Interest and variety can be added to roast poultry and game by using marinades and stuffings. I feel strongly that the stuffing should be an integral part of the meal and not just a filler. Experiment with fruit stuffings for poultry, and use marinades to give flavour to frozen birds.

Since chicken is becoming one of the cheapest meats you have plenty of scope for experimenting with new dishes, and the blender takes the hard work out of stuffings and marinades.

To roast poultry and game

There is nothing more delicious than a simple meal of roasted chicken, pheasant, duck, or turkey. Sometimes a meal of this kind is more difficult for a new cook than a casserole or a dish which seems more complicated but has more explicit instructions in cookbooks. Here is a basic table with cooking times for stuffed poultry and game. In the chart you will find a guide for method and times for open roasting. If you are wrapping in foil then follow cooking times given on the foil packet.

TO ROAST	TEMPERATURE	TIME	PREPARATION
TURKEY	425°F., 220°C., Gas Mark 7 for 15 minutes, reducing to 350°F., 180°C., Gas Mark 4	20 minutes per lb. and 20 minutes over	Stuff the neck with veal forcemeat (see page 32) or chestnut stuffing (see page 38), up to 1 lb. for a 14-lb. bird. Stuff the tail with 1-2 lb. sausagemeat stuffing. Cover the breast with fat bacon. Baste.
GOOSE	425°F., 220°C., Gas Mark 7 for 15 minutes, reducing to 350°F., 180°C., Gas Mark 4	15 minutes per lb. and 15 minutes over	Stuff with sage and onion (see page 29) or a fruit stuffing (see page 39). Baste.
DUCK	400°F., 200°C., Gas Mark 6	20 minutes per lb.	Younger birds do not require stuffing but older, larger ducks are usually stuffed with sage and onion at the tail end. Baste.
CHICKEN	400°F., 200°C., Gas Mark 6	20 minutes per lb. and 20 minutes over	Stuff between the skin and flesh at the wishbone end until the bird is plump. Baste.
PHEASANT	400°F., 200°C., Gas Mark 6 for 15 minutes, reducing to 350°F., 180°C., Gas Mark 4	40–50 minutes for small young birds, 1–1½ hours for larger older birds	Put a knob of butter inside the bird. Baste.
HARE	425°F., 220°C., Gas Mark 7 for 15 minutes, reducing to 375°F., 190°C., Gas Mark 5	1½–2 hours according to size	Stuff the body with veal forcemeat (see page 32).
PIGEON	450°F., 230°C., Gas Mark 8	Centre of the oven for 20–25 minutes. Dredge with flour after 15 minutes.	Stuff with a mixture of 2 tablespoons breadcrumbs, 2 mushrooms, 1 oz. butter, and the chopped pigeon liver. Cover breast with fat bacon. Baste well.

To truss a chicken

After stuffing a bird it is necessary to sew it up so that the stuffing remains inside. Most people buy ready-prepared poultry and game but it is important to know how to truss a bird after it is stuffed as this is one task you complete yourself. If you are intending to do this often it is as well to buy a trussing needle.

Thread a needle with about 18 inches of string. Put the bird on its back, neck end nearest to you, and hold the thighs in an upright position. Put the needle through the top of one thigh behind the joint, bring it through the carcass and out through the other thigh. Turn the bird over then put the needle through the 'elbow' of the wing, bring it over the back and hold down the flap of skin, then bring it out through the other wing elbow. Take the string from the needle, pull the ends tightly, and tie with a double knot.

Now lay the bird on its back again and with about 12 inches of string pass the needle through the skin which is being held over the tip of the breast bone. Unthread and pass the two ends round the thick end of the drumstick, cross the string over the hole, and tie down tightly behind the tail. This means the legs are pulled down over the opening and the breast muscles are plumped up.

❊ Note on frozen poultry

There have been several scares recently about food poisoning caused by eating poultry. The organism which causes this is present in both fresh and frozen poultry but is easily destroyed by ordinary cooking. It is therefore essential to thaw frozen poultry completely before cooking. A partially thawed bird may not allow the heat to penetrate sufficiently to kill off any bacteria which could prove dangerous. Therefore please do ensure that you follow the instructions which are normally on the wrapping of a frozen bird. This is especially important at Christmas when so many people are eating frozen turkeys. It is difficult for me to give an exact thawing time as this depends on the weight. Chicken pieces will therefore defrost more quickly than a whole bird. The best safety precaution is to plan ahead when using frozen poultry and allow it to thaw out overnight in the refrigerator. Do allow sufficient time for birds to cook through when they are being cooked on a spit, barbecue, or grill.

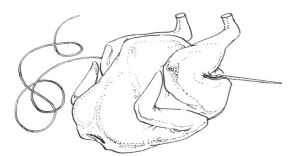

1. Put the needle through thighs behind joints.

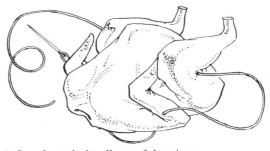

2. Sew through the elbows of the wings.

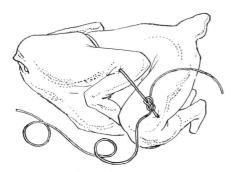

3. Tie tightly with a double knot.

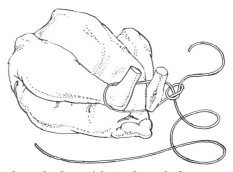

4. Tie down the drumsticks to plump the breast.

APPLE AND CELERY STUFFING

IMPERIAL	AMERICAN
2 oz. butter	¼ cup butter
3 slices streaky bacon	3 slices bacon
2 onions	2 onions
2 stalks celery	2 stalks celery
3 oz. fresh white breadcrumbs	1½ cups fresh white bread crumbs
3 large cooking apples	3 large cooking apples
small bunch parsley sprigs	small bunch parsley sprigs
2 teaspoons sugar	2 teaspoons sugar
salt and pepper	salt and pepper

Melt the butter in a frying pan. Cut the bacon into small pieces and fry until golden brown. Put into a bowl. Fry the roughly chopped onion and celery for a few minutes and in the meantime make the breadcrumbs in the blender. Tip the crumbs into the bowl with the bacon. Peel the apples and slice roughly. Put the onion and celery through the blender until finely chopped while the apples are frying in the frying pan. Add the onions and celery to the mixture in the bowl and lastly put the apples through the blender with the parsley and sugar until finely chopped. Finally mix all ingredients together, season well, and use as a stuffing or cook separately with duck or pork. This stuffing can also be used for a goose but a double quantity will be needed.

CHESTNUT STUFFING

IMPERIAL	AMERICAN
1 lb. fresh chestnuts	1 lb. fresh chestnuts
½ pint milk or chicken stock	1¼ cups milk or chicken stock
4 oz. fresh white bread-crumbs	2 cups fresh white bread crumbs
1 oz. butter	2 tablespoons butter
3 slices lean bacon	3 slices Canadian-style bacon
few sprigs parsley	few sprigs parsley
rind of 1 lemon	rind of 1 lemon
1 egg	1 egg
pinch thyme	pinch thyme
salt and pepper	salt and pepper

Boil the chestnuts for 2 to 3 minutes in water to soften the skins; drain and peel while hot. Simmer for 30 to 40 minutes in milk or chicken stock until soft; drain. While the chestnuts are cooking make the breadcrumbs in the blender and tip into a bowl. Melt the butter and fry the chopped bacon. Put the parsley, lemon rind without pith, egg, and seasoning into the blender and run on high speed until the rind is chopped. Add to the breadcrumbs in the bowl. Place a quarter of the chestnuts in the goblet and switch on at medium speed, add the remainder through the hole in the cap until chestnut purée is obtained. Mix all ingredients together and use to stuff the breast of the turkey.

Variation

Canned whole chestnuts can be used. 8 oz. sausage-meat can be added if only one stuffing is required but many people like to have sausagemeat at one end and chestnut at the other. More beaten egg may be needed to make the stuffing moist.

CHESTNUT AND ORANGE STUFFING

IMPERIAL	AMERICAN
8 oz. fresh white breadcrumbs	4 cups fresh white bread crumbs
2 oranges	2 oranges
15-oz. can chestnuts	15-oz. can chestnuts
4 oz. shredded suet	¾ cup shredded suet
1½ teaspoons salt	1½ teaspoons salt
¼ teaspoon cayenne pepper	¼ teaspoon cayenne pepper
2 eggs	2 eggs

Make the breadcrumbs in the blender. Peel the rind from the oranges thinly and grate in the blender. Squeeze the juice from the oranges and mix all ingredients together using the mixer. This quantity is sufficient for an 8-lb. turkey.

CREAMED SPROUTS

IMPERIAL	AMERICAN
1 lb. sprouts	1 lb. sprouts
4 rashers bacon	4 slices bacon
¼ pint cream	⅔ cup cream
pepper	pepper

Wash the sprouts and boil in salted water for 6 minutes (4 minutes if they are tiny). While the sprouts are cooking, grill the bacon until crisp and keep warm. I try to use the bacon from the pheasant if it is in a good state. Drain the sprouts and put half in the blender, switch on at medium speed until they are chopped. Add the cream and pepper, turn on to medium speed, and add the remaining sprouts one at a time. Reheat and sprinkle with crumbled crispy bacon. Serve with pheasant with grapes. *Serves 4*

PHEASANT WITH GRAPES

IMPERIAL	AMERICAN
1 pheasant	1 pheasant
4 thin slices salt pork or bacon	4 thin slices salt pork or bacon
1½ lb. seedless green grapes	1½ lb. seedless green grapes
¼ pint sour cream	⅔ cup sour cream
1 oz. butter	2 tablespoons butter
1 tablespoon brandy	1 tablespoon brandy
salt and pepper	salt and pepper
20 whole walnuts	20 whole walnuts
1 tablespoon sugar	1 tablespoon sugar
2 tablespoons water	3 tablespoons water
to garnish:	**to garnish:**
grapes	grapes
watercress	watercress

Remove the giblets, season the pheasant, and prepare it for roasting by wrapping in salt pork or bacon (if you buy the pheasant this may have been done by the poulterer); secure with string. Select a small bunch of the best grapes for garnishing. Put the remaining grapes, first removing the stems, in the blender and reduce to a purée. Remove 3 tablespoons of the grape·juice. Add the sour cream, softened butter, brandy, and seasoning to the grapes and blend thoroughly.

Take a deep heavy fireproof casserole or saucepan and lay the walnuts on the bottom. Place the pheasant on top of the walnuts and pour the mixture from the blender on top. Cook gently for about 30 minutes. Put the sugar in a small saucepan with the water and allow to turn to a pale caramel, add the 3 tablespoons reserved grape juice, and pour the mixture over the pheasant. Continue cooking for a further 20 minutes. Meanwhile preheat the oven to 450°F., 220°C., Gas Mark 8 and when the pheasant has finished cooking take it out of the saucepan, remove the pork or bacon, and put it in the oven for a few minutes to brown.

While the bird is in the oven remove the walnuts, allowing them to drain first, and place them in the blender. Allow the sauce to reduce slightly. Chop the walnuts roughly in the blender. Serve the pheasant on a heated serving dish surrounded by chopped walnuts and garnished with grapes; pour the sauce over just before serving.

This is a marvellous dish for a dinner party and it can be partially prepared well in advance. Because you use the blender there is no messy sieving to cause extra washing up. Serve with small roasted potatoes and creamed sprouts.

Serves 4
Cooking time 1 hour
Temperature 450°F., 220°C., Gas Mark 8

CHICKEN HASH

IMPERIAL	AMERICAN
12 oz. cooked chicken	2 cups chopped cooked chicken
10-oz. can condensed chicken soup	10-oz. can condensed chicken soup
2 potatoes	2 potatoes
2 carrots	2 carrots
1 small onion	1 small onion
1 red pepper	1 red sweet pepper
2 sprigs parsley	2 sprigs parsley
sprig rosemary	sprig rosemary
salt and pepper	salt and pepper
crumb topping:	**crumb topping:**
2 slices white bread	2 slices white bread
1½ oz. butter	3 tablespoons butter

Preheat the oven to 350°F., 180°C., Gas Mark 4.

Put the chicken and soup in the blender and run at maximum speed until chicken is finely chopped. Pour into a saucepan and heat. Peel the potatoes and carrots and chop roughly. Put into the blender and run at medium speed until the vegetables are chopped. Add to the chicken mixture. Peel and roughly chop the onion and red pepper and put into the blender with parsley and seasoning. Run on high speed until chopped. Mix all ingredients together in the saucepan, pour into a buttered casserole, and bake for 45 minutes.

Meanwhile make the topping. Clean the blender and use it to make breadcrumbs; mix these with the melted butter. Sprinkle over the baked casserole and cook for a further 10 to 15 minutes.

Serves 6
Cooking time 1 hour
Temperature 350°F., 180°C., Gas Mark 4

Variation

Leftover chicken gravy can be used instead of chicken soup. Serve with tomato sauce (see page 18).

CHICKEN ON THE SPIT

IMPERIAL	AMERICAN
4 chicken portions	4 chicken portions
marinade:	**marinade:**
1 onion	1 onion
7-oz. can tomatoes	7-oz. can tomatoes
1 teaspoon tomato purée	1 teaspoon tomato paste
1 tablespoon lemon juice	1 tablespoon lemon juice
$\frac{1}{4}$ teaspoon rosemary	$\frac{1}{4}$ teaspoon rosemary
1 tablespoon soy sauce	1 tablespoon soy sauce
$3\frac{1}{2}$ tablespoons oil	$\frac{1}{4}$ cup vegetable oil
salt and pepper	salt and pepper
2 tablespoons tomato ketchup	3 tablespoons tomato ketchup

Season the chicken portions and put in a casserole or polythene bag. Roughly chop the onion and put all the ingredients for the marinade into the goblet. Blend until a smooth mixture is obtained. Pour the marinade over the chicken and allow to stand for several hours. ❋ This is an excellent way to use frozen chicken as it can stand in the marinade while it is defrosting. Thread the chicken pieces on the spit and paint generously with the marinade. Cook for 25 to 30 minutes. Paint the chicken with the marinade several times during cooking. Heat the remainder of the marinade with the ketchup and serve hot with the chicken. Serve with rice and a green salad.
Serves 4

FRUITED DUCK OR GOOSE
Illustrated on page 27

IMPERIAL	AMERICAN
1 large duck, about $5\frac{1}{2}$ lb., or 1 small goose, about 7 lb.	1 large duck, about $5\frac{1}{2}$ lb., or 1 small goose, about 7 lb.
stuffing (see page 38)	stuffing (see page 38)
sauce:	**sauce:**
$\frac{1}{4}$ pint seasoned stock made from giblets	$\frac{2}{3}$ cup seasoned stock made from giblets
1 teaspoon Worcestershire sauce	1 teaspoon Worcestershire sauce
16-oz. can pineapple spiral slices	16-oz. can pineapple spiral slices
2 tablespoons sherry	3 tablespoons sherry
2 tablespoons cornflour	3 tablespoons cornstarch
to garnish:	**to garnish:**
12 stuffed green olives	12 stuffed green olives
small bunch parsley	small bunch parsley

Preheat the oven to 400°F., 200°C., Gas Mark 6 (see page 36).

Make up the stuffing and put into both ends of the bird. Place on a trivet in a roasting pan and cook for 2 to $2\frac{1}{2}$ hours in a moderately hot oven, according to size. Remove some of the accumulated fat from the pan, using it to baste the bird if necessary. When it is cooked, place on a hot serving dish and keep warm. Skim off all surplus fat, then pour the pan juices into the blender. Add the stock, Worcestershire sauce, the syrup drained from the pineapple, sherry, and cornflour. Retain three pineapple slices for decoration and add the remainder to the blender goblet. Cover and liquidise until smooth. Pour the mixture into a saucepan, bring to the boil, add the olives, cover, and simmer for 3 minutes. Cut the reserved pineapple slices in half, coat the edges of three halves in finely chopped parsley, and secure over the breast with cocktail sticks topped with olives. Surround the base of the bird with parsley sprigs and the remaining pineapple slices quartered (see photograph on page 27). Serve the sauce separately.
Serves 6
Cooking time 2–$2\frac{1}{2}$ hours
Temperature 400°F., 200°C., Gas Mark 6

CHICKEN PROVENCALE

IMPERIAL	AMERICAN
4 chicken joints	4 chicken joints
2 oz. butter	$\frac{1}{4}$ cup butter
2 cloves garlic	2 cloves garlic
6 large tomatoes, or 15-oz. can peeled tomatoes, drained	6 large tomatoes, or 15-oz. can peeled tomatoes, drained
1 teaspoon tomato purée	1 teaspoon tomato paste
salt and pepper	salt and pepper
2 large sprigs parsley	2 large sprigs parsley
1 teaspoon oregano	1 teaspoon oregano
4 tablespoons sherry	$\frac{1}{3}$ cup sherry

Season the chicken joints and melt the butter in a heavy frying pan; add unpeeled cloves of garlic and the chicken joints. Allow to cook for about 15 minutes. Dip the tomatoes in boiling water one at a time and remove the skins, then put into the blender and chop finely. Add the tomato purée, seasoning, parsley, and oregano, switch on to maximum speed for a few seconds. Heat the sherry in a ladle and set it alight with a match; pour onto the chicken and allow to burn. Add the blended mixture to the chicken and cook for a further 15 to 20 minutes until the chicken is tender and the tomato mixture is reduced. Arrange on a heated serving dish on a bed of rice and coat the chicken with the tomato sauce which is left in the pan. Serve with a crisp green salad.
Serves 4

Egg and cheese dishes

Eggs and cheese are a most important part of a well-balanced diet and with a little imagination they can add enormous variety to our everyday menus as well as saving money. Both products are comparatively cheap in relation to meat and fish, and although they have always been considered as ingredients for quick meals and snacks more people are looking at the possibilities of eggs and cheese in providing main meals. A combination of both can provide a most nutritious and exciting dish and the mixer and blender make even the more complicated dishes simple.

Omelettes

If you enjoy omelettes and pancakes it is wise to keep a pan specially for cooking them as it is important for really successful omelettes to use a pan with a good surface. Frying pans which have been used for bacon, eggs, etc., do tend to lose their surface. To prepare a new omelette pan, heat some oil in the pan until it is smoking hot, then wipe out with a piece of kitchen paper. *Do not wash* after use, simply wipe out with a little salt and kitchen paper. I have had one for eight years and I lock it away from the family and the Brillo pads as I know it will give me perfect omelettes and pancakes.

You can mix a plain omelette in the blender or with the mixer. Use the blender to make fillings and the mixer to make fluffy omelettes.

 PLAIN
OMELETTE

IMPERIAL	AMERICAN
2–3 eggs	2–3 eggs
salt	salt
1 tablespoon water	1 tablespoon water
freshly ground black pepper	freshly ground black pepper
½ oz. butter	1 tablespoon butter

Place all the ingredients except the butter in the blender and switch on to maximum speed for about 15 seconds. Alternatively, use the mixer. Mix the omelette just before cooking for the best results. Divide the butter into small knobs and allow it to melt in the omelette pan on medium heat. When the butter starts to froth pour the egg into the pan and allow the mixture to cook for about 10 seconds. Stir the egg mixture in the pan with the flat part of a fork once or twice, then lift the edge of the omelette to allow any uncooked egg to run onto the pan.

Tilt the pan away from you and fold the omelette over to the other side of the pan. You should now be able to tip the omelette out onto a heated plate by changing your grip on the handle of the pan.
Serves 1

Variations

Prepare the filling before making the omelette. Fillings serve 1.

Cheese omelette Grate 1½ oz. (U.S. ⅓ cup) cheese in the blender. Sprinkle the cheese onto the egg before folding the omelette.

Mushroom omelette Prepare 2 oz. (U.S. ½ cup) mushrooms by washing and slicing them, put into a pan in which a knob of butter has been melted. Allow the mushrooms to sauté for a few minutes then add 1 teaspoon flour, 2 tablespoons water, and seasoning. Stir on the heat until mixture is creamy; add a dash of Worcestershire sauce or a few drops of lemon juice for added flavour. Pour the filling into the omelette before folding.

Tomato and cheese omelette Grate 1 oz. (U.S. ¼ cup) cheese, sauté 1 sliced, seasoned tomato in a little butter. Sprinkle the cheese on the omelette and place the tomato on the far side of the omelette before folding. Cooked diced bacon can be substituted for cheese.

Herb omelette Chop fresh chives and a few sprigs of parsley, thyme, marjoram, or tarragon, depending upon what is available, in the blender and then add to the omelette ingredients and make in the usual way.

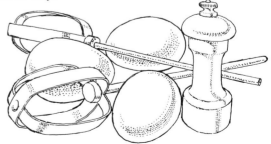

SOUFFLE OMELETTE

IMPERIAL	AMERICAN
2 eggs	2 eggs
salt and pepper	salt and pepper
2 teaspoons water	2 teaspoons water
knob of butter	1 tablespoon butter

Separate the eggs and whisk up the egg whites in the mixer until white and stiff. Season the egg yolks and add the water. Mix together with a fork then fold the yolks into the whites gradually with a sharp-edged metal spoon. Melt the butter in the omelette pan and pour the mixture in. Spread evenly over the pan and cook until almost set; the underside should be golden brown. Put the pan under a preheated grill to brown the top. With a palette knife make a mark across the centre of the omelette and fold over. Slide onto a heated plate.
Serves 1

Variations

Savoury fillings can be added as for plain omelettes. Sweet soufflé omelettes can be made in the same way by adding 2 teaspoons sugar to the egg whites when they are beaten, and omitting the salt and pepper. A little vanilla essence may be added to the yolks. Serve sprinkled with castor sugar. Omelettes can be filled with jam, puréed fruit, or small whole fruit and one omelette will serve two people as a sweet course.

SPANISH OMELETTE

This omelette is not folded over but can be cut into wedges. Cook in a large frying pan.

IMPERIAL	AMERICAN
2 potatoes	2 potatoes
1 large onion	1 large onion
1 clove garlic	1 clove garlic
5 tablespoons oil	6 tablespoons oil
2 oz. lean bacon	3 slices Canadian-style bacon
salt and pepper	salt and pepper
5 eggs	5 eggs
1 tomato	1 tomato

Peel and roughly chop the potatoes, onion, and garlic. Feed them gradually into the blender until they are grated coarsely. Heat the oil in a frying pan, add the bacon, and cook until crisp; remove, allow to cool, and chop in the blender. Put the blender-chopped vegetables in the oil, season, and cook until soft. Pour off any excess oil from the vegetables. Add the bacon. Beat the eggs, pour over the vegetables, and stir until the omelette is just setting. Do not overcook otherwise the egg will be solid. Slice the tomato and place on the omelette, finish cooking under a preheated grill to brown the top, and serve cut into wedges.

This is a very substantial omelette and makes an excellent lunch or supper dish with a crisp salad. Alternatively, serve with a dish of green and red peppers which have been sliced and fried in butter with an onion and a clove of garlic until they are tender.
Serves 4

CHEESE SOUFFLE

IMPERIAL	AMERICAN
1½ oz. butter	3 tablespoons butter
1 oz. flour	¼ cup all-purpose flour
salt	salt
cayenne pepper	cayenne pepper
scant ½ pint milk	1 cup milk
1 teaspoon made mustard	1 teaspoon made mustard
4 oz. grated cheese	1 cup grated cheese
4 egg yolks	4 egg yolks
5 egg whites	5 egg whites

Preheat the oven to 375°F., 190°C., Gas Mark 5. Prepare a 7-inch soufflé dish by buttering it, and if desired sprinkle it with browned breadcrumbs.

Make a roux by melting the butter in a large saucepan, then adding the flour and stirring well. Season well, then blend in the milk with a whisk or put the whole mixture into the blender. Add the mustard and three-quarters of the grated cheese, then the egg yolks one at a time. This operation can all be done in the blender; at this stage return the mixture to the saucepan if using the blender. In the mixer bowl whisk up the egg whites until just stiff. Then fold the whites gradually into the cheese mixture with a sharp-edged metal spoon. Pour into the soufflé dish and sprinkle with remaining cheese. Bake for 25 to 30 minutes in the preheated oven, serve immediately.
Serves 4
Cooking time 25–30 minutes
Temperature 375°F., 190°C., Gas Mark 5

Variation

Pour the mixture over a layer of cooked fish, meat, or vegetables. This is an excellent way of using leftovers.

MUSHROOM SOUFFLE

IMPERIAL	AMERICAN
4 rashers streaky bacon	4 slices bacon
1 medium onion	1 medium onion
4 oz. mushrooms	1 cup sliced mushrooms
1 oz. butter	2 tablespoons butter
4 oz. fresh white bread-crumbs	2 cups fresh white bread crumbs
10½-oz. can condensed mushroom soup	10½-oz. can condensed mushroom soup
salt and pepper	salt and pepper
4 eggs	4 eggs

Preheat the oven to 425°F., 220°C., Gas Mark 7.

Cut the bacon into thin strips. Chop the onion and mushrooms and cook gently with the bacon in the butter for 2 to 3 minutes. Place in a bowl with the breadcrumbs, soup, and seasoning. Mix well together. Separate the eggs and beat the yolks into the mixture one at a time. Place the egg whites in the mixer bowl and whisk on a high speed until just stiff–do not over-whisk as this tends to make them difficult to fold in and the soufflé will not rise well. Fold the egg whites into the mushroom mixture and turn into a 1½-pint (6-inch) buttered soufflé dish or straight-sided deep ovenproof dish and bake in a moderately hot oven for 35 to 40 minutes.

Serves 4
Cooking time 35–40 minutes
Temperature 425°F., 220°C., Gas Mark 7

1. Turning out a roulade

2. Spreading the roulade with filling

3. Rolling the roulade

SPINACH ROULADE

This is a soufflé mixture which is cooked in a Swiss roll tin and rolled like a Swiss roll.

IMPERIAL	AMERICAN
4 eggs	4 eggs
8-oz. packet frozen spinach	8-oz. package frozen spinach
½ oz. butter	1 tablespoon butter
salt and pepper	salt and pepper
1 tablespoon grated Parmesan cheese	1 tablespoon grated Parmesan cheese
filling:	**filling:**
6 oz. mushrooms	1½ cups sliced mushrooms
½ oz. butter	1 tablespoon butter
1 tablespoon flour	1 tablespoon flour
salt and pepper	salt and pepper
¼ pint milk	⅔ cup milk
grated nutmeg	grated nutmeg
2 tablespoons double cream	3 tablespoons whipping cream

Preheat the oven to 400°F., 200°C., Gas Mark 6. Strictly speaking a special paper case is used for a roulade but I find it is just as simple to line a 12- by 8-inch Swiss roll tin as for a Swiss roll with oiled greaseproof paper. Allow 1½-inch side pieces and cut into each corner carefully so that one piece can be folded over the other to form a neat mitre. Brush the paper with oil.

Separate the eggs. Cook the spinach as directed on the packet, drain, and put into the blender to purée, then add the butter, seasoning, cheese, and egg yolks one at a time. In the mixer whisk up the egg whites until white and peaky and fold into the spinach mixture with a metal spoon. Turn into the prepared tin and bake on the top shelf of a moderately hot oven for about 10 minutes or until firm to the touch.

Wash and slice the mushrooms and sauté in the melted butter in a saucepan. Remove from the heat and add the flour. Season and stir in the milk and nutmeg. Return to the heat, stir until thick, and add the cream when the mixture is again removed from the heat. Turn the spinach roulade onto a sheet of greaseproof paper, spread with the mushroom filling, and roll up. It can then be sliced as a first course, or larger portions make a delicious main course.

Serves 4
Cooking time 10 minutes approximately
Temperature 400°F., 200°C., Gas Mark 6

Variation

Meat and fish fillings can be used in place of mushroom.

WHISKY RAREBIT

IMPERIAL	AMERICAN
4 oz. strong Cheddar cheese	1 cup grated sharp Cheddar cheese
1 tablespoon whisky	1 tablespoon whiskey
1 tablespoon milk	1 tablespoon milk
1 teaspoon mustard	1 teaspoon mustard
cayenne pepper	cayenne pepper
1 oz. butter	2 tablespoons butter
2 large slices hot buttered toast	2 large slices hot buttered toast

Put the cheese in the blender to grate coarsely. Add the whisky, milk, mustard, and seasoning and switch on for a few seconds. Melt the butter in a saucepan over a low heat and empty the cheese mixture into the butter. Stir until warm and creamy – do not allow to boil. Pour onto the hot buttered toast. *Serves* 2

Variation

Substitute 2 tablespoons beer for the whisky and milk. Alternatively, use 2 tablespoons milk, omit the whisky and beer, and add a few drops of Worcestershire sauce.

CHEESY BAKED POTATOES

IMPERIAL	AMERICAN
4 large baking potatoes	4 large baking potatoes
8 oz. cottage cheese	1 cup cottage cheese
¼ pint sour cream	⅔ cup sour cream
2 oz. butter	¼ cup butter
4 tablespoons chives	⅓ cup chopped chives
salt and pepper	salt and pepper
1 tablespoon grated cheese	1 tablespoon grated cheese

Scrub the potatoes, mark with a cross, and bake in a hot oven until done (about 1 hour depending on size). Cut the potatoes in half and carefully scoop out some of the insides into the mixer bowl. Add the remaining ingredients except the grated cheese to the bowl and beat well with the mixer. When a smooth mixture is obtained, pile the mixture back into the potatoes and sprinkle with grated cheese. Pop back into the oven to heat.

These potatoes are marvellous as a snack if you are not on a diet and also delicious served with steaks or chops.
Serves 4
Cooking time 1 hour approximately
Temperature 400°F., 200°C., Gas Mark 6

EGGS WITH SPINACH

IMPERIAL	AMERICAN
11 oz. packet frozen spinach	11-oz. package frozen spinach
4 oz. Cheddar cheese	1 cup grated Cheddar cheese
4 eggs	4 eggs
4 tablespoons single cream	⅓ cup coffee cream
salt and pepper	salt and pepper

Preheat the oven to 350°F., 180°C., Gas Mark 4.

Cook the spinach as directed, drain, and cool. Divide between four buttered ramekin dishes. Grate the cheese in the blender. Break a whole egg carefully into each ramekin dish, put 1 tablespoon cream over each egg, season, and sprinkle with **grated cheese**. Place the dishes in a roasting tin which is quarter-filled with warm water and bake in a moderate oven for 25–30 minutes.
Serves 4
Cooking time 25–30 minutes
Temperature 350°F., 180°C., Gas Mark 4

SAVOURY ROLLS

IMPERIAL	AMERICAN
filling:	**filling:**
4 oz. cooked chicken	½ cup chopped cooked chicken
few sprigs parsley	few sprigs parsley
½ onion	½ onion
knob of butter	1 tablespoon butter
batter:	**batter:**
2 eggs	2 eggs
¼ pint water	⅔ cup water
salt	salt
2 oz. plain flour	½ cup all-purpose flour
topping:	**topping:**
2 oz. grated cheese	½ cup grated cheese

Put the chicken, parsley, and peeled and roughly chopped onion in the blender and chop finely. Empty into a saucepan in which the butter has been melted and cook gently until the rolls are ready. Put the eggs, water, and salt in the blender and switch on at high speed, then add the flour gradually while the blender is on. Rub the omelette pan over with oil, heat, then pour in a little batter to coat the bottom of the pan. When the underside is golden, turn out onto kitchen paper, cooked side up. Fill with the hot filling, fold the sides in, and roll up. When all the rolls are done, arrange in a serving dish, sprinkle with grated cheese, and brown under the grill. *Serves* 4

Hot puddings and cold sweets

Every family has a few favourite sweets and puddings but with the mixer and blender to take all the labour out of even the most elaborate party sweets, you can be more ambitious. Astound your friends with soufflés and meringues and the family with featherlight sponge puddings. Interesting textures and lovely toppings all add to the pleasure of making delicious puddings and sweets.

HOT SWISS TRIFLE
Illustrated on page 55

IMPERIAL	AMERICAN
1 Swiss roll	1 jelly roll
1 small can apricots	1 small can apricots
2 tablespoons custard powder	3 tablespoons cornstarch few drops vanilla extract
2 eggs, separated	2 eggs, separated
sugar	sugar
1 pint milk	2½ cups milk

Preheat the oven to 350°F., 180°C., Gas Mark 4, and prepare a buttered ovenproof dish.

Slice the Swiss roll and arrange around the sides of the dish, together with the apricots. Mix the custard powder, egg yolks, and 1 to 2 tablespoons sugar with a little of the milk; put the remainder on to heat. When nearly boiling pour onto the custard mixture, stir well, and return to the saucepan. Stirring all the time bring to the boil. Pour into the dish.

Whisk the egg whites stiffly then continue whisking while adding 3 to 4 tablespoons sugar. Pile on top of the custard. Bake in the centre of the oven for about 20 minutes.
Serves 6
Cooking time 20 minutes
Temperature 350°F., 180°C., Gas Mark 4

LEMON SUNSHINE PUDDINGS

IMPERIAL	AMERICAN
4 oz. fresh white breadcrumbs	2 cups fresh white bread crumbs
2 oz. suet	⅓ cup shredded suet
4 oz. castor sugar	½ cup sugar
grated rind and juice of 1 lemon	grated rind and juice of 1 lemon
1 egg, beaten	1 egg, beaten

Make the breadcrumbs in the blender with fresh white bread. Add the suet and sugar to the breadcrumbs and switch on for a second. Add lemon rind, juice, and egg and blend for a few seconds.

Transfer the mixture into four individual ¼-pint plastic or foil pudding basins. Cover securely with lid, foil, or double greaseproof paper and steam or boil for 30 minutes. Turn out and serve hot with cream.
Serves 4

ZABAGLIONE

IMPERIAL	AMERICAN
4 egg yolks	4 egg yolks
2 oz. castor sugar	¼ cup sugar
5 tablespoons Marsala or sweet sherry	6 tablespoons Marsala or sweet sherry

Whisk the egg yolks with the hand mixer until fluffy. Add the sugar and Marsala and beat the mixture in a bowl over a pan of hot water until it is thick, creamy, and the whisk leaves a trail. If using a stand mixer there is no need to whisk over hot water.

Serve at once in individual glasses, with sponge fingers.
Serves 4

1. Heat a strong frying pan (not too large) rubbed over with oil or dripping until it is smoking hot. Pour a small ladle of batter into the pan. Turn the pan until the bottom is coated. When the pancake is nicely browned flip it over, brown the other side, and slip onto a plate.

2. Pancakes can be used immediately or you will probably find it more convenient to pile them on a plate and keep them warm in the oven. Leave them uncovered if you do this. Spread the apricot purée on each pancake and roll up, place on a heated serving dish.

3. Arrange the filled pancakes on the serving dish, decorate with halved apricots, and pour over the apricot glaze before serving.

APRICOT PANCAKES

IMPERIAL	AMERICAN
4 oz. plain flour	1 cup all-purpose flour
pinch salt	pinch salt
1 egg	1 egg
1 tablespoon oil	1 tablespoon oil
$\frac{1}{2}$ pint milk	1$\frac{1}{4}$ cups milk
little oil to cook	little oil to cook
2$\frac{1}{2}$-lb. can apricot halves, drained	2$\frac{1}{2}$-lb. can apricot halves, drained
$\frac{1}{2}$ pint apricot juice	1$\frac{1}{4}$ cups apricot juice
3 teaspoons arrowroot	3 teaspoons arrowroot flour

Sieve the flour and salt into the mixer bowl. Make a well in the centre and drop in the egg and oil. Switch the mixer on at medium speed and gradually add the milk to form a smooth batter. Heat a strong frying pan or omelette pan rubbed over with oil or dripping until it is smoking hot. Pour a small ladle of mixture into the pan and turn the pan until the mixture coats the bottom. Shake when mixture looks cooked or lift one corner with a palette knife. When nicely browned flip over, allow the other side to become golden, and slip onto a plate. Pile the cooked pancakes on a plate and keep warm in the oven.

Blend the apricot halves in the blender, reserving a few for decoration. To make the sauce, blend a little of the apricot juice with the arrowroot, bring the remainder to the boil. Pour onto the arrowroot and return to the pan; bring to the boil stirring well. Pile a little of the apricot purée on half of each pancake, fold the other half over, and arrange on an ovenproof dish. Decorate with the remaining apricots and pour a little sauce over each.
Makes 8–10

BLENDER PANCAKES

IMPERIAL	AMERICAN
batter:	**batter:**
scant $\frac{1}{2}$ pint milk	1 cup milk
rind and juice of 1 orange	rind and juice of 1 orange
3 eggs	3 eggs
4 oz. plain flour	1 cup all-purpose flour
$\frac{1}{4}$ teaspoon salt	$\frac{1}{4}$ teaspoon salt
filling:	**filling:**
orange brandy butter (see page 22)	orange brandy butter (see page 22)
juice of 2 oranges	juice of 2 oranges
2 tablespoons brandy	3 tablespoons brandy
1 tablespoon castor sugar	1 tablespoon sugar

Pour the milk into the goblet, add the orange rind, cover, and blend until the rind is finely grated. Add the remaining ingredients and blend on medium speed until smooth, about 30 seconds. Heat the omelette pan and pour some of the mixture onto the pan until a thin pancake is formed. Cook until golden brown on each side. Fill with a spoonful of brandy butter, roll up, and keep warm on a heated serving dish.

Warm the orange juice, brandy, and sugar in a saucepan and pour over the pancakes just before serving.

Serves 4–6

FRUIT FRITTERS

IMPERIAL	AMERICAN
fritter batter:	**fritter batter:**
2 oz. plain flour	½ cup all-purpose flour
good pinch salt	good pinch salt
4 tablespoons warmed water	⅓ cup warmed water
2 teaspoons salad oil	2 teaspoons salad oil
1 egg white	1 egg white

Put the flour, salt, water, and oil into the blender, switch on at medium speed, and blend until a smooth batter is obtained. Beat the egg white until stiff and fold the blended mixture into the egg white with a metal spoon.

Apple fritters Peel and core medium-sized apples and cut into ½-inch slices. Dust lightly with flour, dip into the batter, drain, and fry in hot oil until golden brown on both sides. Sprinkle with a mixture of cinnamon and castor sugar.

Pineapple fritters Cut thin rings of fresh pineapple and prepare as for apple fritters. Canned fruit may also be used.

Banana fritters Cut small bananas in half lengthwise and halve across the middle. Dip the bananas in lemon juice or lemon juice and rum, and treat as for apple fritters.

APPLE CRUMBLE

IMPERIAL	AMERICAN
1 lb. apples	1 lb. apples
1 teaspoon allspice	1 teaspoon allspice
4–6 oz. castor sugar	½–¾ cup sugar
8 oz. plain flour	2 cups all-purpose flour
5 oz. butter	⅔ cup butter
5 oz. castor sugar	⅔ cup sugar

Preheat the oven to 375°F., 190°C., Gas Mark 5.

Peel and core the apples, slice thinly, and arrange in a greased pie dish in layers sprinkled with allspice and sugar. Soft brown sugar can be used with apples in place of castor sugar. Sieve the flour into the mixer bowl, add the butter, and mix into the flour until the butter is in small lumps. Add the 5 oz. sugar and mix well. Sprinkle evenly over the fruit and level the surface with a palette knife. Bake on the middle shelf of the oven for 15 minutes then reduce the temperature to 350°F., 180°C., Gas Mark 4 for a further 30 minutes. Serve with whipped cream, pouring cream, or custard sauce (see page 22).

Serves 6
Cooking time 45 minutes
Temperature 375°F., 190°C., Gas Mark 5, reducing to 350°F., 180°C., Gas Mark 4

Variation

Plums, gooseberries, apple and blackcurrant, or rhubarb can be used. Omit the allspice. Crumble mixture can be made up in large quantities and stored in an airtight jar in the fridge for some weeks. ❊ Crumble can be frozen cooked or raw.

APPLE PUDDING

IMPERIAL	AMERICAN
2 apples	2 apples
4 oz. walnuts	1 cup walnuts
2 eggs	2 eggs
5 oz. plain flour	1¼ cups all-purpose flour
½ teaspoon salt	½ teaspoon salt
2½ teaspoons baking powder	2½ teaspoons baking powder
1 teaspoon vanilla essence	1 teaspoon vanilla extract
12 oz. brown sugar	1½ cups brown sugar, firmly packed

Preheat the oven to 375°F., 190°C., Gas Mark 5.

Peel and slice the apples, drop into the blender, and chop roughly. Spread apples on the bottom of an ovenproof dish. Drop the nuts into the blender at low speed and chop into fairly small pieces. Empty into a bowl. Put the remaining ingredients into the blender and blend at medium speed for 1 to 1½ minutes, scraping the mixture down from time to time. Mix well with the nuts, then turn onto the apples and spread over the dish. Bake in a moderate oven.

Serves 6
Cooking time 35 minutes
Temperature 375°F., 190°C., Gas Mark 5

Note: This is only suitable for a large blender.

UPSIDE-DOWN APPLE CAKE

IMPERIAL	AMERICAN
1 large cooking apple	1 large cooking apple
2 tablespoons soft brown sugar	3 tablespoons brown sugar
1 oz. whipped-up vegetable fat	2 tablespoons whipped-up shortening
4 oz. castor sugar	½ cup sugar
4 oz. butter or margarine	½ cup butter or margarine
2 eggs	2 eggs
4 oz. self-raising flour	1 cup all-purpose flour sifted with 1 teaspoon baking powder
1 tablespoon warm water	1 tablespoon warm water

Preheat the oven to 350°F., 180°C., Gas Mark 4.

Peel and core the apple, slice thinly. Grease a deep 8-inch tin, preferably one with a loose bottom. Mix the brown sugar with the fat in a small saucepan over low heat until the fat and sugar are combined; the fat should not be allowed to become oily. Spread this mixture over the bottom of the tin. Arrange the apple in rings starting at the outside of the tin until the bottom of the tin is covered with a neat pattern of apple slices. Cream the fat and sugar in the mixer until light in colour and creamy in texture. When the mixture is creamed sufficiently it will drop off the end of the beaters easily. Add the eggs one by one; a teaspoon of flour can be added with the second egg to prevent the mixture curdling. Add the sieved flour and fold in lightly with a metal spoon. Add 1 tablespoon warm water to the mixture before turning out of the bowl over the apples. Bake in a moderate oven for 40 minutes. Allow to cool slightly then carefully turn out onto a wire tray. Serve with whipped cream, custard sauce (see page 22), or ice cream as a dessert, or decorate with cream and use at tea time.

Serves 6
Cooking time 40 minutes
Temperature 350°F., 180°C., Gas Mark 4

Variation

5 rings of canned pineapple or sliced canned peaches may be substituted for the apple.

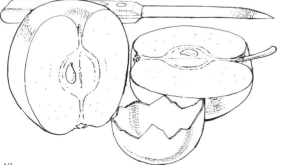

1. This picture shows the apples being arranged on top of the brown sugar mixture. If there is a delay in making the cake put the sliced apple in lemon juice to avoid excessive browning.

2. The fat and sugar have been creamed and the eggs beaten into the mixture. Scrape down the sides of the bowl and turn out onto the apple mixture.

3. Here is the finished upside-down cake which has been carefully removed from the tin so that the apple slices remain undisturbed.

Upside-down cakes can be decorated with cherries and piped cream. Pineapple cakes usually have a cherry in the centre of each pineapple ring.

STEAMED SPONGE PUDDING

IMPERIAL	AMERICAN
4 oz. margarine	½ cup margarine
4 oz. castor sugar	½ cup sugar
2 eggs	2 eggs
6 oz. plain flour	1½ cups all-purpose flour
2 tablespoons water	3 tablespoons water
½ teaspoon salt	½ teaspoon salt
½ level teaspoon baking powder	½ teaspoon double-acting baking powder

Cream the fat and sugar with the mixer until pale and creamy. Add one egg and continue beating; add 1 teaspoon flour and then add the remaining egg. Add the slightly warmed water and mix well, scraping the bowl down. Sieve the flour, salt, and baking powder and fold in with a metal spoon. Put in a greased 1½-pint pudding bowl and steam for 1½ hours. Alternatively, steam in a pressure cooker as directed by the manufacturers – usually about 25 minutes under 5-lb. pressure. Serve with warmed syrup or lemon sauce (see page 22).
Serves 4

Variations

Lemon or orange rind can be added to the basic mixture and 1 tablespoon of either juice can replace 1 tablespoon of the water.

Cherry pudding 3 oz. glacé cherries (U.S. ⅓ cup candied cherries) can be added with the flour.

Chocolate pudding Make 1 oz. (U.S. 2 tablespoons) rice into flour with the blender, add 1 oz. (U.S. ¼ cup) cocoa to it, and substitute for 2 oz. (U.S. ½ cup) of the measured flour.

Coconut pudding Add 3 oz. desiccated (U.S. 1 cup shredded) coconut with the flour.

Ginger pudding Add 2–3 oz. (U.S. ⅓ cup chopped) preserved ginger and ½ teaspoon ground ginger with the flour.

Fruit pudding Add 3 oz. (U.S. ½ cup) sultanas (seedless white raisins), raisins, or currants.

Apricot pudding Stone and slice 1 lb. apricots and place in an ovenproof dish in layers with 4 oz. (U.S. ½ cup) sugar. Make up the steamed sponge mixture and spread over the apricots. Bake for 45 to 60 minutes in a moderate oven (350°F., 180°C., Gas Mark 4). Serve with cream. Gooseberries, rhubarb, or apples are equally good.

CHRISTMAS PUDDING

IMPERIAL	AMERICAN
8 oz. white breadcrumbs	4 cups white bread crumbs
6 oz. suet	1 cup plus 3 tablespoons shredded suet
6 oz. brown sugar	¾ cup brown sugar, firmly packed
4 oz. plain flour	1 cup all-purpose flour
½ teaspoon salt	½ teaspoon salt
1 teaspoon baking powder	1 teaspoon double-acting baking powder
½ teaspoon mixed spice	½ teaspoon mixed spice
¼ teaspoon nutmeg	¼ teaspoon nutmeg
8 oz. currants	1⅓ cups currants
8 oz. sultanas	1⅓ cups seedless white raisins
6 oz. raisins	1 cup raisins
2 oz. peel	⅓ cup candied peel
1 oz. ground almonds	¼ cup ground almonds
rind of 1 lemon	rind of 1 lemon
4 eggs	4 eggs
½ pint old ale	1 cup dark beer

Make the breadcrumbs in the blender and empty into a large bowl. Shred the suet in the blender and add to the breadcrumbs, add the sugar, and mix well. Sieve the flour, salt, baking powder, and spice into the bowl with the breadcrumbs. Add the cleaned fruit, ground almonds, and lemon rind. The raisins and lemon rind can be chopped in the blender if using large raisins. Mix all together with the mixer adding the eggs and ale gradually until the ingredients are well mixed together. Grease three 2-pint (U.S. 5-cup) pudding bowls and fill three-quarters full with the mixture. Cover well with a lid, two layers of greaseproof paper, or a clean cloth, and steam for 8 hours. Alternatively cook one by one in a pressure cooker where they will take about 3 to 4 hours at 15 lb. of pressure and about 40 to 50 minutes to reheat, but check the weights of the puddings with the instructions given with the pressure cooker. Serve with a hard sauce (see page 22).
Serves 14–16

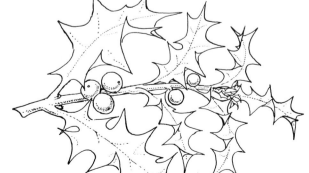

COFFEE SOUFFLE

IMPERIAL	AMERICAN
1 oz. flour	¼ cup all-purpose flour
1 oz. butter	2 tablespoons butter
¼ pint milk	⅔ cup milk
2 tablespoons coffee essence	3 tablespoons coffee extract
1½ oz. castor sugar	3 tablespoons sugar
3 egg yolks	3 egg yolks
4 egg whites	4 egg whites

Preheat the oven to 350°F., 180°C., Gas Mark 4. Grease a 6-inch soufflé dish.

Make a roux in a saucepan by stirring the flour and butter together over a low heat for a few minutes. Add the milk and coffee essence and cook until thick. Should the sauce form lumps put it into the blender to smooth. Add the sugar, allow to cool slightly, and add the egg yolks one at a time. Whisk the egg whites with the mixer until stiff, fold carefully into the yolk mixture with a sharp-edged metal spoon. Make sure all the white is mixed in before pouring into the dish and baking on the middle shelf of the oven for 30 to 40 minutes.
Serves 4
Cooking time 30–40 minutes
Temperature 350°F., 180°C., Gas Mark 4

LEMON MERINGUE PIE

IMPERIAL	AMERICAN
blender pastry (see page 66)	blender pastry (see page 66)
filling:	**filling:**
3 eggs, separated	3 eggs, separated
8 oz. castor sugar	1 cup sugar
3 lemons	3 lemons
1½ oz. cornflour	6 tablespoons cornstarch
½ pint water	1 cup water

Preheat the oven to 400°F., 200°C., Gas Mark 6.

Make the pastry in the blender as directed on page 65. Use to line an 8-inch flan ring and bake blind. Cool. To make the filling, place the egg yolks in a bowl with 3 oz. of the castor sugar and whisk with the mixer over hot water until creamy. Grate the rind from two lemons, squeeze the juice from all three, and place in a saucepan. Moisten the cornflour with a little of the water, put the remainder of the water in the saucepan, and bring to the boil. Pour onto the cornflour, return to the saucepan, and cook, stirring, until thick. Cool. Whisk in the egg yolks and sugar, allow to cool, then use to fill the baked flan case. Place the egg

whites in the mixer bowl and whip with the mixer until stiff, fold in 1 tablespoon sugar with a metal spoon, pile meringue on top of filling, and place in a moderately hot oven until the meringue begins to crisp on top.
Serves 6
Cooking time pastry 15 minutes, meringue 10 minutes
Temperature 400°F., 200°C., Gas Mark 6

Variation

Fruit meringue pie Fill the flan case with stewed fruit, e.g., apples or apples and blackberries. Top with meringue, see apple meringue on the cover.

BITTER ORANGE CHEESECAKE
Illustrated opposite

IMPERIAL	AMERICAN
1½ oz. butter	3 tablespoons butter
3 oz. digestive biscuits	1 cup graham cracker crumbs
1 dessertspoon sugar	1 tablespoon sugar
4 oz. chocolate	4 squares semi-sweet chocolate
1 orange jelly	4-oz. package orange-flavored gelatin
2 medium oranges	2 medium oranges
12 oz. cream cheese	1½ cups cream cheese

Melt the butter in a small saucepan. Place the biscuits a few at a time in the blender goblet and run the machine until reduced to fine crumbs. Grease a 6- to 7-inch deep cake tin with a loose base. Mix the crumbs with the butter and sugar then press into the base of the tin. Melt 3 oz. of the chocolate in a bowl over hot water; pour over the biscuit base, spreading evenly, and leave until set.

Divide the jelly into cubes, place in the blender with ¼ pint (U.S. ⅔ cup) boiling water, and run the machine at high speed to dissolve the jelly; pour into a bowl. Cut each orange into four pieces and put into the liquidiser gradually with ¼ pint cold water; run for a short time at high speed.

Strain into the jelly then return all to the blender; gradually add the cream cheese and run until well blended. Half set the jelly then pour onto the biscuit base. When set, push up the base of the tin, carefully remove the base, and place the cheesecake on a serving dish.

To decorate, melt the remaining chocolate and place in a greaseproof paper icing bag, cutting off the tip. Pipe a design on top of the cheesecake as illustrated on page 51, finishing with a slice of orange. *Serves* 6

Raspberry cooler (page 53), gooseberry fool (page 53), and bitter orange cheesecake

LEMON CHEESECAKE

IMPERIAL	AMERICAN
crumb crust:	**crumb crust:**
2 oz. butter	¼ cup butter
3 oz. biscuit crumbs	1 cup graham cracker crumbs
2 oz. sugar	¼ cup sugar
¼ teaspoon cinnamon	¼ teaspoon cinnamon
filling:	**filling:**
8 oz. curd cheese	1 cup curd cheese
8 oz. cream cheese	1 cup cream cheese
½ pint double cream	1¼ cups whipping cream
3 egg yolks	3 egg yolks
9 tablespoons lemon juice	¾ cup lemon juice
grated rind of 1 lemon	grated rind of 1 lemon
4 oz. sugar	½ cup sugar
1 tablespoon cornflour	1 tablespoon cornstarch
3 egg whites	3 egg whites

Preheat the oven to 300°F., 150°C., Gas Mark 2.

Melt the butter in a saucepan, remove from the heat, and stir in the biscuit crumbs, sugar, and cinnamon. Press into the base of an 8-inch loose-bottomed tin. Cool.

Place curd and cream cheeses, cream, egg yolks, lemon juice, rind, sugar, and cornflour in the blender and run at medium speed until smooth. Transfer to a bowl. Whisk the egg whites until stiff using the mixer and gently fold into the cheese mixture. Pour the mixture on top of the crumb crust and bake in a cool oven for 1½ hours, until set. Allow to cool completely, preferably overnight, and turn out.
Serves 8
Cooking time 1½ hours
Temperature 300°F., 150°C., Gas Mark 2

ORANGE AND CINNAMON PIE

Illustrated on page 55

IMPERIAL	AMERICAN
2 oz. butter	¼ cup butter
4 oz. plain flour	1 cup all-purpose flour
1 oz. castor sugar	2 tablespoons sugar
1 oz. chopped walnuts	¼ cup chopped walnuts
1 teaspoon ground cinnamon	1 teaspoon cinnamon
1 egg, separated	1 egg, separated
water	water
1 packet orange instant whip	1 package instant orange pudding mix
½ pint milk	1¼ cups milk
to decorate:	**to decorate:**
angelica	candied angelica
candied orange segments	candied orange segments

Heat the oven to 400°F., 200°C., Gas Mark 6. Have ready a 7-inch flan ring or loose-bottomed sandwich tin.

Rub the butter into the flour and add the sugar, chopped walnuts, and cinnamon. Mix to a stiff dough with a mixture of egg yolk and water. Knead lightly and roll out into a round about 9 inches in diameter. Line the flan ring, prick the base with a fork, and bake it in the middle of the oven for about 15 to 20 minutes. Cool.

Just before serving make up the instant whip as directed on the packet. Stiffly whisk the egg white and stir it lightly through the whip. Turn this into the baked case and serve decorated with angelica and candied orange sections (see page 55).
Serves 6
Cooking time 15–20 minutes
Temperature 400°F., 200°C., Gas Mark 6

PINEAPPLE WATER-LILY PUDDING

Illustrated on page 27

IMPERIAL	AMERICAN
16-oz. can pineapple cubes	16-oz. can pineapple cubes
1 packet lemon jelly	4-oz. package lemon-flavored gelatin
8 white marshmallows	8 white marshmallows
6-oz. can evaporated milk	6-oz. can evaporated milk
1 teaspoon lemon juice	1 teaspoon lemon juice
few drops green food colouring	few drops green food coloring
few slices angelica	few slices candied angelica

Strain the syrup from the pineapple cubes into a measuring jug and make up to ½ pint (U.S. 1¼ cups) with water. Bring to boiling point, add the jelly, and stir until dissolved. Reserve half the quantity for the top of the mousse, leave in a warm place as it should not set too quickly. Dissolve 4 marshmallows in the remaining jelly. Liquidise the pineapple cubes, reserving a few for decoration. Put the evaporated milk and lemon juice in a bowl and whisk with the mixer on high speed until it will form soft peaks. Fold in the pineapple. Stir this mixture into the half-set jelly, mix lightly, turn into a bowl, and chill. Tint the remaining jelly green with a few drops of food colouring. If necessary, place the container in warm water for a few minutes first. Run the tinted jelly over the surface of the mousse. When this jelly topping has set, decorate with the remaining marshmallows, snipped round the edge to look like lilies with scissors dipped in icing sugar. Put a tiny piece of pineapple in the centre of each flower, and a leaf of angelica at the side as shown in the photograph on page 27.
Serves 6

GOOSEBERRY FOOL
Illustrated on page 51

IMPERIAL	AMERICAN
$\frac{1}{4}$ pint thick custard, unsweetened	$\frac{2}{3}$ cup thick custard, unsweetened
1 lb. 3-oz. can gooseberries	1 lb. 3-oz. can gooseberries
juice of $\frac{1}{2}$ lemon	juice of $\frac{1}{2}$ lemon
2 tablespoons double cream	3 tablespoons whipping cream
1 egg white	1 egg white

Make the custard and allow to cool. Place the gooseberries and juice in the blender and blend until smooth. Sieve the purée into a bowl to remove the seeds, reserving $\frac{1}{4}$ pint (U.S. $\frac{2}{3}$ cup) for the decoration. Rinse out the goblet and pour in the remaining purée, custard, lemon juice, and cream; blend well. Divide between three or four glasses.

Whisk the egg white stiffly with the mixer and fold in the reserved gooseberry purée. Swirl on top of the gooseberry fool in each glass (see page 51).
Serves 3–4

RASPBERRY SOUFFLE

IMPERIAL	AMERICAN
6 oz. sugar	$\frac{3}{4}$ cup sugar
4 tablespoons water	$\frac{1}{3}$ cup water
6 egg yolks	6 egg yolks
$\frac{1}{2}$ pint double cream	$1\frac{1}{4}$ cups whipping cream
2 oz. castor sugar	$\frac{1}{4}$ cup sugar
8 oz. raspberries	$1\frac{1}{2}$ cups raspberries

Tie a band of greased paper around a 7-inch soufflé dish to come at least 1 inch above the edge of the dish. Put the sugar and water in a saucepan and boil until a syrup is formed. The syrup is ready when a long thread is formed when a spoon is dipped in the mixture. Put the egg yolks in a bowl over hot water and turn on the hand mixer. Add the syrup slowly while the mixer is running at medium speed. Cook for about 40 to 45 minutes in the double boiler until a thin sauce consistency is reached. Whip the cream until thick and add the castor sugar. Blend the raspberries until puréed, add to the whipped cream. Combine the two mixtures and pour into the prepared soufflé dish. Put the dish into the cold part of the refrigerator or the freezer. Remove from the freezer 15 minutes before required and serve decorated with fresh raspberries if available.
Serves 6

RASPBERRY WATER ICE

IMPERIAL	AMERICAN
6 oz. granulated sugar	$\frac{3}{4}$ cup sugar
$\frac{1}{3}$ pint water	generous $\frac{3}{4}$ cup water
2 lb. raspberries	2 lb. raspberries
3 tablespoons icing sugar	$\frac{1}{4}$ cup sifted confectioners' sugar
$\frac{1}{2}$ egg white, whisked	$\frac{1}{2}$ egg white, whipped

Make a sugar syrup by dissolving the sugar in the water over a gentle heat. Allow to cool. Put the raspberries in the blender, blend until a purée is formed, add the icing sugar, and blend well. Pour in the cold sugar syrup, blend again. Sieve into ice trays and chill in the freezing compartment of a refrigerator or in the freezer. Do not allow the mixture to become hard. Whisk the egg white until stiff, return the chilled mixture to the blender and mix well, add the egg white. Return to the freezer, stir from time to time until the mixture is set. Serve decorated with raspberries and leaves. ❄ If you make a lot of ice cream you can now buy a small electric machine to go inside the freezer which stirs the ice cream all the time.
Serves 4

Variation

Pineapple water ice Substitute 1 large pineapple, peeled and cored, for the raspberries and purée in the blender to yield about $\frac{3}{4}$ pint (U.S. 2 cups).

RASPBERRY COOLER
Illustrated on page 51

IMPERIAL	AMERICAN
15-oz. can raspberries	15-oz. can raspberries
$\frac{1}{2}$ pint milk	$1\frac{1}{4}$ cups milk
2–3 sprigs fresh mint	2–3 sprigs mint
to decorate:	**to decorate:**
mint leaves	mint leaves

Place the raspberries and juice in the blender goblet and run at top speed for a few seconds. Sieve the purée into a bowl. Rinse out the goblet, pour in the purée, milk, and mint, and run the machine until well blended. ❄ Pour the mixture into the ice trays or a bowl and place in the freezing compartment of the refrigerator, or place in the freezer.

Leave until just beginning to freeze, return to the blender, and mix until smooth. Replace in the freezing compartment and leave until frozen. Serve scoops or spoonfuls in glasses and decorate with mint leaves as illustrated on page 51.
Serves 4

RASPBERRY SHORTCAKE
Illustrated opposite

IMPERIAL	AMERICAN
8 oz. butter	1 cup butter
6 oz. castor sugar	¾ cup sugar
12 oz. plain flour	3 cups all-purpose flour
¼ pint milk	⅔ cup milk
1 packet raspberry Angel Delight	1 package raspberry-flavored whipped dessert mix
1 raspberry yogurt	1 raspberry yogurt
to decorate:	**to decorate:**
icing sugar	sifted confectioners' sugar
raspberries	raspberries

Heat the oven to 325°F., 170°C., Gas Mark 3 and have ready two baking sheets.

Beat the butter and sugar together until white and creamy; work in the flour. Knead the mixture lightly and shape into two flat rounds about 8 inches in diameter.

Place on separate baking sheets, crimp the edges, prick one well with a fork, and mark the other into eight wedge-shaped pieces. Bake towards the bottom of the oven for 30 to 40 minutes. Sprinkle with castor sugar before quite cold.

Put the milk in a bowl, whisk in the raspberry Angel Delight, then stir in the yogurt. Put the shortcake base on the serving dish, swirl with the raspberry mixture, and arrange the shortcake wedges on top dusted alternately with icing sugar and castor sugar. Decorate with fresh or frozen raspberries.

Serves 8
Cooking time 30–40 minutes
Temperature 325°F., 170°C., Gas Mark 3

CHOCOLATE MOUSSE

IMPERIAL	AMERICAN
6 oz. plain chocolate	1 cup semi-sweet chocolate pieces
rind and juice of 1 orange	rind and juice of 1 orange
4 eggs	4 eggs
to decorate:	**to decorate:**
whipped cream	whipped cream
grated chocolate	grated chocolate

Put the chocolate and orange rind in the blender and chop finely. Empty into a bowl and place over a saucepan of hot water, making sure that the water does not touch the bowl. Add the orange juice to the chocolate and allow to melt. Meanwhile separate the eggs. Remove the bowl from the heat

and stir in the egg yolks one at a time. Whisk the egg whites until stiff, fold into the chocolate mixture, and pour into a serving dish or four individual pots. Allow to chill and decorate with whipped cream and melted chocolate.
Serves 4

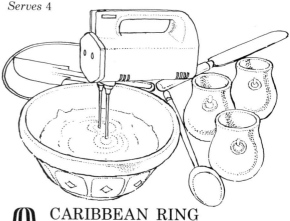

CARIBBEAN RING
Illustrated on page 59

IMPERIAL	AMERICAN
4 oz. butter	½ cup butter
6 oz. plain chocolate	1 cup semi-sweet chocolate pieces
4 oz. castor sugar	½ cup sugar
4 eggs, separated	4 eggs, separated
1 teaspoon vanilla essence	1 teaspoon vanilla extract
1 level teaspoon baking powder	1 teaspoon double-acting baking powder
small packet instant mashed potato	small package instant mashed potato
large can fruit salad	large can fruit salad
¼ pint double cream	⅔ cup whipping cream

Preheat the oven to 350°F., 180°C., Gas Mark 4. Grease a 3-pint ring tin (U.S. 2-quart tube pan).

Melt the butter in a saucepan. Add the chocolate, broken into pieces, and stir over a gentle heat until melted. Remove the pan from the heat. Stir in the sugar. Beat in the egg yolks with a hand mixer, then add the vanilla essence, sifted baking powder, and the potato. Whisk the egg whites until stiff and fold into the chocolate mixture. Turn into the prepared tin and bake in a moderate oven for 35 to 40 minutes, until cooked. Turn out on a wire rack to cool.

Put the cake on a large plate. Drain off the liquid from the canned fruit and pile the fruit into the centre. Lightly whip the cream and fill a piping bag with a star pipe attached. Pipe five rosettes on the top and more round the base. Serve as a special pudding or cake.
Serves 6
Cooking time 35–40 minutes
Temperature 350°F., 180°C., Gas Mark 4

Orange and cinnamon pie (page 52), raspberry shortcake, coffee mallow gâteau (page 61), and hot Swiss trifle (page 45)

Baking

Here the mixer comes into its own in a really big way, taking the hard work out of so many tasks – from kneading dough for bread to whipping up the lightest, fluffiest sponge you've ever tasted. Pastry can be made in the mixer or in the blender, as you like.

Cakes and pastries can be made in one step using the mixer. Whipped-up margarines and shortenings make these a great success. Grandmother may be horrified by such new-fangled sleight of hand but what a boon to busy mothers who have children's teas and family puddings to provide. ❋ Cakes freeze very well.

 WHITE BREAD

IMPERIAL	AMERICAN
yeast liquid:	**yeast liquid:**
½ oz. fresh yeast	½ oz. compressed yeast
¾ pint water	scant 2 cups water
or	**or**
2 teaspoons dried yeast	2 teaspoons active dry yeast
1 teaspoon sugar	1 teaspoon sugar
¾ pint warm water	scant 2 cups warm water
dry mixture:	**dry mixture:**
1½ lb. plain flour	6 cups all-purpose flour
1 teaspoon salt	1 teaspoon salt
½ oz. lard	1 tablespoon shortening

Either blend the fresh yeast with the water, or dissolve the sugar in the water and sprinkle on the dried yeast. If using dried yeast allow to stand until frothy, about 10 minutes.

Sieve the flour and salt into the mixer bowl and rub in the lard. Pour in the yeast liquid and knead well with the dough hook until the mixture leaves the sides of the bowl clean, adding a very little extra flour if needed. Continue kneading with the dough hook until the dough is no longer sticky.

Place the dough in a lightly greased large polythene bag loosely tied, or in the mixer bowl covered with polythene or a damp tea towel. Allow to rise until doubled in size and the dough springs back when pressed with a floured finger.

Rising times are adaptable to fit in with your plans but the best results are achieved by a slow rise.

Warm place: 45 to 60 minutes – quick rise
Room temperature: 2 hours – slower rise
Cold larder or room: up to 12 hours – slow rise
Refrigerator: up to 24 hours – very slow rise

Dough which has been risen in the refrigerator must be allowed to return to room temperature before shaping.

Turn the risen dough onto a lightly floured board and flatten firmly with the knuckles to knock out the air bubbles, then knead to make the dough firm and ready for shaping.

For a large loaf, stretch the dough into an oblong the same width as a 2-lb. loaf tin, fold into three, turn in ends, and place in the greased tin. For 2 small loaves, divide the dough in half, shape as for a large loaf, and place in two 1-lb. loaf tins.

Put the dough to rise again, by placing the tins inside a lightly greased polythene bag and allowing the dough to come to the top of the tin. It should spring back when pressed with a floured finger. Leave for 1 to 1½ hours at room temperature or longer in a refrigerator.

Heat the oven to 450°F., 230°C., Gas Mark 8. Remove the polythene and bake the loaves in the centre of a hot oven for 30 to 40 minutes until well risen and golden brown. Remove from the tins and cool on a wire tray.

Cooked loaves sound hollow when tapped underneath and shrink slightly from the sides of the tin.
Cooking time 30–40 minutes
Temperature 450°F., 230°C., Gas Mark 8

❋ **Note:** Bread can be frozen successfully if wrapped and sealed immediately it is completely cold. Thaw at room temperature allowing 2 to 3 hours for a large loaf. Bread can be thawed in the oven but tends to stale more quickly. Sliced bread can be toasted whilst still frozen.

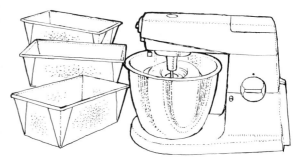

WHOLEMEAL BREAD

IMPERIAL	AMERICAN
1¾ oz. fresh yeast	1¾ oz. compressed yeast
1½ pints tepid water	3¾ cups tepid water
3 lb. wholemeal flour	12 cups wholewheat flour
¾ oz. salt	1½ tablespoons salt
1 oz. fat	2 tablespoons shortening

Mix the yeast with half the tepid water. Mix the flour and salt together in the mixer bowl, make a well in the middle, and pour in the yeast mixture and the melted fat. Using the dough hook, gradually mix all ingredients together, adding the remaining water. Knead well with the dough hook until the dough is no longer sticky. Put the dough to rise in a greased polythene bag, mixer bowl, or greased saucepan with a lid for about 35 to 60 minutes in a warm place until it has doubled its size. Knead to knock out air.

Divide the dough into 6 portions and shape into rolls. Place in lightly greased 1-lb. loaf tins or on greased baking sheets. Allow to rise again for at least 30 to 40 minutes. Heat the oven to 450°F., 226°C., Gas Mark 8. Bake in a hot oven for about 30 minutes.

Makes 6 loaves
Cooking time 30 minutes
Temperature 450°F., 220°C., Gas Mark 8

PIZZA

IMPERIAL	AMERICAN
½ lb. white dough which has had one rising	½ lb. white dough which has had one rising
olive oil for brushing	olive oil for brushing
filling:	**filling:**
1 oz. Cheddar cheese	¼ cup grated Cheddar cheese
7-oz. can peeled tomatoes	7-oz. can peeled tomatoes
1 tablespoon tomato purée	1 tablespoon tomato paste
1 small clove garlic	1 small clove garlic
½ teaspoon fresh or dried thyme, oregano, marjoram, or basil	½ teaspoon fresh or dried thyme, oregano, marjoram, or basil
8 anchovy fillets	8 anchovy fillets
few black olives	few ripe olives

Roll the risen dough into a long strip. Brush with oil and roll up like a Swiss roll. Repeat this three times. Oil two 6-inch sandwich tins, or one 12- by 8-inch Swiss roll tin. Divide dough if necessary, roll to fit tin, press in with the knuckles, and brush with oil. To make the filling, grate the cheese.

Place the drained tomatoes, tomato purée, crushed garlic, and herbs in the blender and using a slow speed mix until blended. Cover the pizza dough with alternate layers of tomato mixture and cheese, finishing with a layer of cheese. Place anchovies and stoned and halved black olives on top and allow to stand in a cool place for about 30 minutes. Meanwhile heat the oven to 450°F., 230°C., Gas Mark 8. Bake for 20 to 30 minutes.

Serves 4
Cooking time 20–30 minutes
Temperature 450°F., 230°C., Gas Mark 8

✤ **Note:** Pizza freezes extremely well either in the uncooked state or cooked. The pizza can be frozen after the filling has been added or after cooking. Children love pizza but probably without the anchovies and olives. I substitute small rolls of bacon or cooked ham.

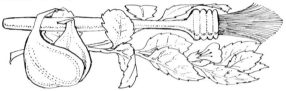

OVEN SCONES

IMPERIAL	AMERICAN
8 oz. self-raising flour	2 cups all-purpose flour
2 teaspoons baking powder	4 teaspoons double-acting baking powder
pinch salt	pinch salt
1 tablespoon castor sugar	1 tablespoon sugar
2 oz. margarine	¼ cup margarine
¼ pint milk	⅔ cup milk

Preheat the oven to 425°F., 220°C., Gas Mark 7.

Sieve all the dry ingredients into the mixer bowl and cut the margarine into small pieces. Switch on the beater until the fat is rubbed into the flour. Add the milk and knead the mixture for a few minutes with the beater; do not over-knead, however. Turn onto a floured board, roll out with a lightly floured rolling pin, cut into rounds with a cutter. Put the rounds on a greased baking sheet in the oven for about 10 to 12 minutes depending on the thickness of the scones.

Makes 10
Cooking time 10–12 minutes
Temperature 425°F., 220°C., Gas Mark 7

Variation

Cheese scones Omit sugar, add 3 tablespoons grated cheese and a good pinch of dry mustard before adding the milk.

DROPPED
SCONES

IMPERIAL	AMERICAN
8 oz. self-raising flour	2 cups all-purpose flour
2 teaspoons baking powder	4 teaspoons double-acting baking powder
pinch salt	pinch salt
1 oz. castor sugar	2 tablespoons sugar
1 egg	1 egg
generous ¼ pint milk	¾ cup milk

Sieve the flour, baking powder, and salt in the mixer bowl. Sprinkle in the castor sugar. Make a well in the centre, drop in the egg and at least half of the milk. Switch on the mixer and beat until a smooth batter is obtained. Stir in the remaining milk with a metal spoon and allow to stand in a cool place for at least 15 minutes before using. Preheat a girdle or thick frying pan slowly on a moderate heat. Grease with a piece of dripping or cooking fat. Drop four dessertspoons of mixture onto the girdle, allow bubbles to appear all over the surface before turning to allow top side to brown. Place in a clean tea towel or kitchen paper on a wire tray until cool.
Makes 24

 PLAIN SPONGE
CAKE

IMPERIAL	AMERICAN
3 eggs	3 eggs
3 oz. castor sugar	6 tablespoons sugar
3 oz. plain flour	¾ cup all-purpose flour
pinch baking powder	pinch baking powder

Preheat the oven to 350°F., 180°C., Gas Mark 4. Use ingredients at room temperature and warm the bowl and whisk slightly before using. Grease and flour a 6-inch tin which is 3 inches deep, or two 8-inch sandwich tins.

Break the eggs into the bowl, add the sugar, and whisk until the mixture is thick, very pale yellow, and fluffy. Remove the bowl from the machine, sieve in half the flour and baking powder, fold in with a metal spoon. Add the other half of the flour and fold in carefully. Turn into the prepared tin. Cook for 45 to 50 minutes in the deep tin; sandwich tins take 20 minutes at 400°F.

Turn the cake out carefully onto a wire tray and allow to cool. Sandwich together with jam, sieve icing sugar on top. Alternatively fill with whipped cream and fresh or canned fruit.
Cooking time 45–50 minutes or 20 minutes
Temperature 350°F., 180°C., Gas Mark 4, or 400°F., 200°C., Gas Mark 6

 SWISS
ROLL

IMPERIAL	AMERICAN
2 oz. self-raising flour	½ cup all-purpose flour sifted with ½ teaspoon baking powder
2 large eggs	2 eggs
2 oz. castor sugar	¼ cup sugar
3 tablespoons jam	¼ cup jam

Preheat the oven to 425°F., 220°C., Gas Mark 7.
Sieve the flour and warm for a few minutes. Prepare a 6- by 10-inch tin by lining with greaseproof paper. Allow enough to line the sides, cut into the corners, and mitre neatly. Warm the bowl and whisk for a few moments. Put the eggs in the bowl with the sugar, and whisk until the mixture is pale yellow and thick. Sieve the flour into the egg mixture and fold in with a metal spoon. Pour into the prepared tin. Cook on the second top shelf of the oven for 7 to 8 minutes. Turn out onto a piece of greaseproof paper cut the same size as the Swiss roll tin, which has been sprinkled with castor sugar. Trim the edges of the sponge, spread with warmed jam, and roll up tightly. Dust with castor or icing sugar.
Cooking time 7 minutes
Temperature 425°F., 220°C., Gas Mark 7

Variation

The Swiss roll can be rolled without filling, then when it is cool unrolled and filled with whipped cream or butter icing (see page 67).
Party cakes Swiss rolls can be used as a base for several party cakes.
Yule log The most common one is the yule log when the roll is decorated on the outside with chocolate butter icing (see page 67) or melted chocolate. To suit the season a robin or sprig of holly will add the finishing touch for tea time around Christmas.
Engine cake The roll can be decorated with butter icing and liquorice all-sorts used as wheels and chimneys. Small children like the coal truck filled with smarties. This can be made by piping or arranging the icing with a knife into a small square at the back of the engine, then filling with sweets, see illustration below.

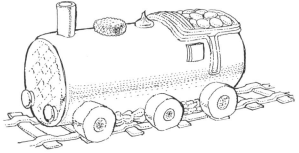

Small cakes and wizard wonder (page 60), and Caribbean ring (page 54)

WIZARD WONDER

Illustrated on page 59

IMPERIAL	AMERICAN
6 oz. self-raising flour	1½ cups all-purpose flour
2 level tablespoons cocoa	3 tablespoons unsweetened cocoa powder
1 level teaspoon baking powder	2½ teaspoons double acting baking powder
6 oz. soft margarine	¾ cup soft margarine
6 oz. castor sugar	¾ cup fine sugar
3 eggs	3 eggs
topping:	**topping:**
3 oz. glacé cherries	⅓ cup candied cherries
1½ oz. walnut halves	⅓ cup walnut halves
2 rounded tablespoons apricot jam	¼ cup apricot jam

Preheat the oven to 350°F., 180°C., Gas Mark 3. Grease a 2-lb. loaf tin. Make a lining using a double strip of greaseproof paper cut to fit the width of the tin and protruding at either end. Grease this paper lining also.

Sieve the dry ingredients together into a bowl, add the margarine, sugar, and eggs, and cream thoroughly with the mixer until the mixture is well blended. Spoon into the prepared tin, smoothing over the surface, and hollow out the centre. Bake the cake in a warm oven for 1½ hours. Test with a skewer; the cake is cooked when the skewer comes out clean.

While the cake is cooking, prepare the topping. Halve the cherries and walnuts and put into a pan with the jam. Stir continuously, bring to the boil, and cook. Pour over the cake and leave in the tin until cold. Lift the cake out using the ends of the paper to help.

Cooking time 1½ hours
Temperature 350°F., 180°C., Gas Mark 3

Variation

Small cakes Cook the mixture in a lined Swiss roll tin at the top of a moderately hot oven (400°F., 200°C., Gas Mark 6) for about 10 minutes. Turn out and allow to cool, then cut into shapes as shown in the pictures opposite. Decorate with butter icing (see page 67).

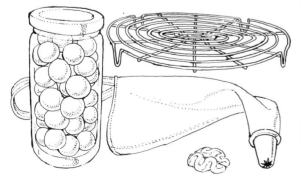

1. Sieve the dry ingredients together into a bowl, add the margarine, sugar, and eggs. Switch on and mix well. Put into the prepared Swiss roll tin and cook for 10 minutes.

2. Turn out onto a wire tray, allow the cake to cool thoroughly. Using shaped cutters, cut the chocolate cake into crescents, rounds, and squares. Prepare the butter icing (see page 67).

3. Cut the cakes in half. Spread with butter icing, cream, or jam. Sandwich together and decorate using a piping bag and nozzle.

COFFEE MALLOW GATEAU

Illustrated on page 55

IMPERIAL	AMERICAN
plain sponge cake (see page 58)	plain sponge cake (see page 58)
12 marshmallows	12 marshmallows
$\frac{1}{5}$ pint black coffee	$\frac{1}{2}$ cup black coffee
1 sachet dream topping	1 2-oz. package whipped topping mix
$\frac{1}{5}$ pint milk	$\frac{1}{2}$ cup milk
chopped nuts	chopped nuts
crystallised violets	crystallized violets

Make the sponge cake mixture according to the directions on page 58 and put in an 8-inch deep cake tin. Bake at 350°F., 180°C., Gas Mark 4 for 45 to 50 minutes. Turn out carefully and allow to cool.

Put the marshmallows and coffee in a small saucepan and melt gently. Leave to cool and thicken. Make up the dream topping with milk as directed on the packet and lightly stir in the coffee mixture. Split the cake through the centre and sandwich it together with one third of the coffee mallow mixture.

Assemble the gâteau by swirling most of the remaining coffee mallow mixture on top and around the sides of the cake leaving a little for the piped rosettes. Decorate the sides of the gâteau with chopped nuts and the top with rosettes and crystallised violets (see photograph page 55).

Cooking time 45–50 minutes

Temperature 350°F., 180°C., Gas Mark 4

FUDGE CAKE

IMPERIAL	AMERICAN
1 oz. stoned raisins	$2\frac{1}{2}$ tablespoons seedless raisins
$2\frac{1}{2}$ oz. glacé cherries	$\frac{1}{3}$ cup candied cherries
3 tablespoons golden syrup	$\frac{1}{4}$ cup corn syrup
4 oz. butter	$\frac{1}{2}$ cup butter
2 tablespoons drinking chocolate	3 tablespoons sweetened cocoa powder
8 oz. wholemeal biscuits	$\frac{1}{2}$ lb. graham crackers
few chocolate buttons	few chocolate buttons

Grease and line a 1-lb. loaf tin, using a double strip of greaseproof paper to fit the width of the tin and protruding at either end. Grease the paper. Soak the raisins in warm water for a few minutes, drain. Place the raisins in the blender. Reserve 4 cherries and place remainder in blender. Run on high speed until fruit is chopped, place in bowl. Place the biscuits in the blender and blend until mixture looks like breadcrumbs; place in bowl with fruit. Melt the syrup and butter in a saucepan, add the drinking chocolate, and pour over the dry ingredients. Press the mixture into the prepared tin; decorate the top with the remaining cherries and chocolate drops. Leave overnight then carefully lift out of the tin using the paper strips.

CHOCOLATE ORANGE CAKE

IMPERIAL	AMERICAN
2 oz. plain chocolate	2 squares semi-sweet chocolate
6 oz. butter	$\frac{3}{4}$ cup butter
6 oz. castor sugar	$\frac{3}{4}$ cup sugar
3 large eggs	3 large eggs
5 oz. plain flour	$1\frac{1}{4}$ cups all-purpose flour
1 oz. cocoa	$\frac{1}{4}$ cup unsweetened cocoa powder
pinch salt	pinch salt
$\frac{1}{4}$ pint double cream	$\frac{2}{3}$ cup whipping cream
1 tablespoon milk	1 tablespoon milk
3 oranges	3 oranges
2 oz. granulated sugar	$\frac{1}{4}$ cup sugar
4 tablespoons water	$\frac{1}{3}$ cup water

Preheat the oven to 350°F., 180°C., Gas Mark 4.

Melt the chocolate in a small bowl over a pan of hot water, spread on a cool marble or Formica surface, and allow to harden. Make chocolate curls by pushing a sharp knife away from you over the surface of the chocolate.

Cream the butter and sugar together in the mixer bowl, beat in the egg yolks. Sieve together the flour, cocoa, and salt and fold in lightly. Whisk the egg whites until stiff and fold into the mixture. Turn into a greased and base-lined deep 8-inch cake tin and bake in a moderate oven for about 50 minutes. Cool on a wire tray then slice into four equal layers.

Whisk the cream and milk together. Thinly peel the zest from one orange, then remove the skin and pith from all three oranges and cut the flesh into segments. Dissolve the remaining sugar in the water, add the orange peel, then boil until a thick syrup is formed. Remove from the heat.

To assemble the cake, spread the bottom layer of cake with half the cream, place the second layer on top, and arrange orange segments over. Add the third layer, spread with remaining cream, and top with the last layer of cake. Spoon the glaze over the cake, decorate with chocolate curls, and dust with icing sugar.

This cake may be served as a sweet.

Cooking time 50 minutes

Temperature 350°F., 180°C., Gas Mark 4

FRUIT CAKE

IMPERIAL	AMERICAN
8 oz. butter	1 cup butter
4 oz. castor sugar	½ cup sugar
4 oz. brown sugar	½ cup brown sugar, firmly packed
1 tablespoon treacle	1 tablespoon molasses
5 eggs	5 eggs
2 tablespoons brandy	3 tablespoons brandy
10 oz. plain flour	2½ cups all-purpose flour
½ teaspoon allspice	½ teaspoon allspice
½ teaspoon cinnamon	½ teaspoon cinnamon
1 lb. currants	2⅔ cups currants
8 oz. sultanas	1⅓ cups seedless white raisins
4 oz. chopped peel	⅔ cup chopped candied peel
4 oz. glacé cherries	½ cup candied cherries
2 oz. chopped almonds	½ cup chopped almonds
grated rind of 1 lemon	grated rind of 1 lemon

Preheat the oven to 300°F., 150°C., Gas Mark 2.

Cream the butter and sugars together in the mixer bowl until light and fluffy, using the mixer on medium speed. Gradually beat in the treacle and then the eggs, one at a time, adding a little flour with the last addition if necessary. Beat in the brandy. Sieve the flour with the spices and fold into the mixture; finally add the fruit, folding in gently with a metal spoon. Grease and line an 8-inch cake tin and tie a band of brown paper round the outside. Place the mixture in the baking tin, stand on a piece of brown paper in the oven, and bake for 3 to 4 hours.

Cooking time 3–4 hours
Temperature 300°F., 150°C., Gas Mark 2

ORANGE CARAMEL CAKE

IMPERIAL	AMERICAN
6 oz. butter	¾ cup butter
6 oz. castor sugar	¾ cup sugar
grated rind of 1 orange	grated rind of 1 orange
3 eggs	3 eggs
6 oz. self-raising flour	1½ cups all-purpose flour sifted with 1½ teaspoons double-acting baking powder
orange butter icing (see page 67)	orange butter icing (see page 67)
to decorate:	**to decorate:**
few crystallised orange segments	few candied orange segments

Preheat the oven to 375°F., 190°C., Gas Mark 5. Grease and line two 8-inch sandwich tins.

Warm the mixer bowl and cream together the butter, sugar, and orange rind on a medium speed for about 2 minutes until the mixture is light and fluffy. Reduce the speed to low and add the eggs one at a time. Turn speed to high and beat well for 20 to 30 seconds, scraping down sides if necessary. Switch to low speed and add the flour, switching off immediately the flour is mixed in. Divide the mixture between prepared tins and bake for about 25 minutes; turn onto a wire tray and allow to cool.

Sandwich the cakes together with a little of the butter icing, spread the remainder over the top and sides of the cake, and decorate with the orange segments.

Cooking time 25 minutes
Temperature 375°F., 190°C., Gas Mark 5

CHOUX PASTRY

IMPERIAL	AMERICAN
¼ pint water	⅔ cup water
2 oz. butter	¼ cup butter
2½ oz. plain flour	½ cup plus 2 tablespoons all-purpose flour
½ teaspoon salt	½ teaspoon salt
2 teaspoons sugar	2 teaspoons sugar
2 eggs	2 eggs

Pour the water into a saucepan, add the butter, allow to melt, and then bring to the boil. *Do not boil for too long before adding the flour.* Sieve the flour and salt onto a paper, sprinkle with sugar. Tip the flour into the boiling liquid and beat with a wooden spoon until the mixture becomes very thick and leaves the side of the pan. Allow the thick mixture to cool slightly, place in the mixer bowl. Switch on at a low speed and add the eggs one at a time. This beating process is very important as the lightness of the paste will depend on how much air is incorporated at this stage. To beat by hand is a very tiring process but the mixer makes it very easy. Beat in each egg thoroughly then switch the mixer to maximum speed for 30 seconds and the choux pastry is ready for use.

Preheat the oven to 400°F., 200°C., Gas Mark 6. Prepare a greased baking sheet and a ½-inch meringue pipe in a forcing bag.

Chocolate éclairs Fill the forcing bag with the choux pastry. Hold the bag so that it is lying almost parallel with the baking sheet and force the pastry out in 2½-inch lengths. Cut away from the pipe with a wet knife; leave about 1½ inches space between each éclair. Bake in the centre of the preheated oven for 20 to 30 minutes. The éclairs should be

Pineapple cider cup (page 78), salmon and cucumber dip (page 8), cheese and pineapple dip (page 8), and tuna dip (page 8)

crisp, golden brown, and dried through. Test by tapping the base – the pastry should sound hollow. Alternatively split them open; if there is any soggy inside return to the oven for a few minutes. Allow to cool, then fill with whipped cream. Dip the top into or coat with chocolate topping made by melting 2-4 oz. plain chocolate (U.S. $\frac{1}{3}$–$\frac{2}{3}$ cup semi-sweet chocolate pieces) with 1 oz. (U.S. 2 tablespoons) butter over hot water, or coffee glacé icing.

Cream puffs Pipe or spoon onto a greased baking sheet in small rounds. Puffs will take 25 to 35 minutes to cook depending on the size. Allow to cool, fill with whipped cream, and dredge with icing sugar. Puffs may be used as a sweet, then they can be filled with fresh or canned fruit with cream.

Savoury choux buns Small savoury choux buns can be made by omitting the sugar from the mixture. Pipe smaller rounds for excellent cocktail savouries. Fill with a little white sauce mixed with shrimps, mushrooms, chicken, salmon. The cottage cheese and chive mixture used in the baked potatoes recipe (see page 44) is also an excellent filling. The salmon or tuna dip (see page 8) can also be used as a filling.

❆ **To freeze choux pastry** Choux pastry can be frozen baked or unbaked. To freeze unbaked pipe onto trays, open freeze for about 1 hour, then pack in foil, polythene boxes or bags. The frozen shapes can go straight from the freezer into the oven but allow an extra 5 minutes on the cooking time. The pastry shapes can be stored for about 3 months.

To freeze baked choux pastry, pack unfilled in a polythene bag or foil then in a polythene box. To use remove from the freezer and stand at room temperature for about 1 hour then pop into a moderate oven (350°F., 180°C., or Gas Mark 4) for five minutes; cool and fill. Baked shells will keep frozen for at least 6 months.

❆ **Notes on freezing pastry**

All baked or unbaked pastry freezes well. Short crust pastry takes about 3 hours to thaw before it can be rolled therefore I can see little advantage in freezing it in a lump. It is much better to shape it into flans, pies, or tartlet cases before freezing either baked or unbaked.

Fruit or meat pies can be made in foil dishes,

plates, or flan rings. Put into the freezer uncovered but do not make holes or vents for the steam to escape otherwise the filling tends to dry out. When the pies are hard cover with heavy duty foil. Small pies can be removed from tins and stored in foil, polythene bags, or boxes.

Flan cases can be frozen in the rings or foil cases until hard; then remove rings, wrap in foil, and pack in a polythene box. Unbaked pastry stores well for 3 months.

To cook frozen shaped pastry Pies can be unwrapped and placed in a preheated oven; bake at the usual temperature allowing extra time for thawing. Cut vents on the top as the pastry thaws.

Flan cases will take about 25 minutes to bake 'blind' from the frozen state.

Cooked pastry pies and flans should be cooled quickly, left in the dishes, and packed in heavy duty foil. Freeze immediately when cool. Meat and fish pies will keep well for about 3 months, fruit pies last well for up to 5 or 6 months, unfilled pastry cases for about 6 months. Allow pies to thaw at room temperature for 2 hours before reheating.

 SHORT CRUST PASTRY

IMPERIAL	AMERICAN
2 oz. butter or margarine	$\frac{1}{4}$ cup butter or margarine
2 oz. white cooking fat	$\frac{1}{4}$ cup lard
8 oz. plain flour	2 cups all-purpose flour
1 teaspoon salt	1 teaspoon salt
4 tablespoons cold water	$\frac{1}{3}$ cup cold water

Cut the fat into pieces and put in the mixer bowl, switch on at minimum speed. Tip the sieved flour and salt into the bowl and slightly increase the speed until the fat is broken up. Allow to mix until the mixture becomes like breadcrumbs; add the water and mix for only a few seconds until a dough is obtained. Turn out of the bowl onto a lightly floured board and use for either sweet or savoury dishes.

Variations

Sweet short crust Increase the fat content to 5 oz. (U.S. $\frac{2}{3}$ cup) and put in the bowl with 2 teaspoons castor sugar. Mix the pastry with 1 egg yolk and 1 tablespoon water.

Cheese pastry Use 3 oz. (U.S. 6 tablespoons) fat and make as directed, adding a pinch of cayenne pepper and dry mustard to the flour. When the mixture is like breadcrumbs, add 2 oz. (U.S. $\frac{1}{2}$ cup) grated cheese. Mix well and bind with 2 tablespoons cold water.

ONION FLAN

IMPERIAL	AMERICAN
quick-mix pastry:	**quick-mix pastry:**
6 oz. plain flour	1½ cups all-purpose flour
½ teaspoon salt	½ teaspoon salt
3 oz. whipped-up cooking fat	6 tablespoons whipped-up shortening
1½ tablespoons water	2 tablespoons water
filling:	**filling:**
1 lb. onions	1 lb. onions
1½ oz. butter	3 tablespoons butter
1 tablespoon olive oil	1 tablespoon olive oil
2 eggs	2 eggs
¼ pint double cream	⅔ cup whipping cream
salt and pepper	salt and pepper

Preheat the oven to 400°F., 200°C., Gas Mark 6.

Put all pastry ingredients into the mixer bowl and blend at minimum speed until pastry forms one piece. With soft fat this will happen in a very short time. Turn out onto a floured board, roll out, and line an 8-inch pie plate or flan ring. Prick the bottom of the flan, fill with baking beans, and cook on the second top shelf of the oven for 15 minutes.

Meanwhile, cut the peeled onions into rings and sweat in the butter and oil until transparent and soft–do not brown. Beat the eggs with the cream, season well. Arrange the onions in the flan and cover with the cream and egg mixture. Bake in a moderate oven until golden brown. This flan is delicious hot or cold and makes a marvellous hot starter on its own.

Serves 4–6

Cooking time approximately 35 minutes

Temperature 350°F., 180°C., Gas Mark 4

Variations

Quiche lorraine Beat 1 egg and 1 egg yolk in a bowl with 1 oz. (U.S. ¼ cup) grated cheese, ¼ pint (U.S. ⅔ cup) milk, and seasoning. Melt ½ oz. (U.S. 1 tablespoon) butter in a saucepan and slowly cook 2–3 slices bacon, chopped, and 1 small onion, chopped, until golden brown. Add to the egg mixture, pour into the pastry case, and cook as for onion flan.

Bacon, egg, and tomato flan Mix 2 eggs, 2 oz. (U.S. ½ cup) grated cheese, 2 tablespoons milk or thin cream, and salt and pepper with 2–3 slices bacon, chopped and cooked, and pour into the pastry case. Cover with sliced tomatoes and cook until set.

1. Sieve the salt and flour into the bowl, cut the shortening roughly into the flour, and turn the mixer on at the slowest speed. Add the water and mix to a firm consistency. Do not overmix or the pastry will be difficult to roll out.

2. Turn the pastry out onto a lightly floured board and form a round shape. Roll out using firm strokes with a lightly floured rolling pin. Turn the pastry continually to retain the round shape. When it is a little larger than the flan ring lift the pastry on the rolling pin, line the ring, and roll firmly as shown in the picture to trim the edge of the flan. Fill and bake as directed.

3. The finished flan may be eaten on its own as a first course, or served as a supper dish with salad.

BLENDER PASTRY

IMPERIAL	AMERICAN
8 oz. plain flour	2 cups all-purpose flour
½ teaspoon salt	½ teaspoon salt
4 oz. margarine or soft cooking fat	½ cup shortening
2 tablespoons cold water	2–3 tablespoons cold water

Put the flour, salt, and fat into the blender. Switch on for about 10 seconds. Stop and scrape down the sides of the blender with a wooden spatula. Tip out onto the table, make a well in the centre, and add 1 tablespoon water; when this is absorbed add the remaining water. If this seems too difficult tip crumb mixture into a bowl, add the water, and mix with a fork. Allow to rest in the refrigerator for a few minutes before using.

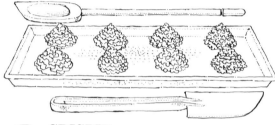

CRISPIE BARS

IMPERIAL	AMERICAN
2½ oz. plain flour	⅔ cup all-purpose flour
1 oz. castor sugar	2 tablespoons sugar
2 oz. butter	¼ cup butter
topping:	**topping:**
1 oz. margarine	2 tablespoons margarine
1 tablespoon golden syrup	1 tablespoon corn syrup
1 tablespoon sugar	1 tablespoon sugar
1 tablespoon cocoa	1 tablespoon unsweetened cocoa powder
1 oz. rice krispies	1 cup rice krispies

Preheat the oven to 350°F., 180°C., Gas Mark 4.

Sieve the flour and sugar into the mixer bowl and using the mixer on medium speed rub in the butter. Knead lightly until mixture holds together. Roll into a 7-inch square and bake in a moderate oven for about 12 minutes; cool.

Put margarine, syrup, sugar, and cocoa into a saucepan and stir over low heat until dissolved. Add the krispies and turn in the mixture until completely coated. Spread the topping over the shortbread and allow to set. Cut into bars when quite cold.
Makes 14
Cooking time 12 minutes
Temperature 350°F., 180°C., Gas Mark 4

COCONUT HEAPS

IMPERIAL	AMERICAN
3 oz. butter	6 tablespoons butter
3 oz. castor sugar	6 tablespoons sugar
1 egg	1 egg
4 oz. plain flour	1 cup all-purpose flour
1 tablespoon cocoa	1 tablespoon unsweetened cocoa powder
1 teaspoon baking powder	1 teaspoon double-acting baking powder
2 oz. desiccated coconut	⅔ cup shredded coconut
1 tablespoon milk	1 tablespoon milk
filling:	**filling:**
butter icing (see page 67)	butter icing (see page 67)

Preheat the oven to 375°F., 190°C., Gas Mark 5.

Cream the butter and sugar together in the mixer bowl, then add the egg, beating well. Sieve together the flour, cocoa, and baking powder and fold into the mixture. Stir in the coconut and mix to a soft dough with the milk. Place teaspoonfuls of the mixture on greased baking sheets and bake in a moderately hot oven for about 15 minutes. Cool on a wire tray. Sandwich together in pairs with the butter icing.
Makes 12
Cooking time 15 minutes
Temperature 375°F., 190°C., Gas Mark 5

SHORTBREAD

IMPERIAL	AMERICAN
8 oz. butter	1 cup butter
4 oz. castor sugar	½ cup sugar
8 oz. plain flour	2 cups all-purpose flour
4 oz. rice flour	1 cup rice flour

Preheat the oven to 375°F., 190°C., Gas Mark 5.

Mix the butter and sugar together with the mixer until light and creamy then, using the mixer on a slow speed, gradually work in the flour until the mixture holds together. Knead the dough lightly with the hands and form into two 8-inch cakes on a greased baking sheet, or press into two greased 8-inch loose-bottomed sandwich tins. Pinch the edges and prick all over with a fork. Put into a fairly hot oven and bake for 20 minutes until pale golden.
Cooking time 20 minutes
Temperature 375°F., 190°C., Gas Mark 5

MARMALADE COOKIES

IMPERIAL	AMERICAN
4 oz. margarine	½ cup margarine
4 oz. castor sugar	½ cup sugar
2 eggs	2 eggs
2 tablespoons chunky marmalade	3 tablespoons chunky marmalade
1 oz. drinking chocolate	¼ cup sweetened cocoa powder
7 oz. self-raising flour	1¾ cups all-purpose flour, sifted with 2 teaspoons double-acting baking powder
2 oz. rolled oats	good ½ cup rolled oats

Preheat the oven to 400°F., 200°C., Gas Mark 6.

Cream the margarine and sugar together in the mixer bowl then add the eggs one at a time, beating well. Add the marmalade. Sieve together the drinking chocolate and flour and fold into the mixture lightly using a metal spoon. Roll teaspoons of the mixture in the oats and place on greased baking sheets. Bake in a moderately hot oven for about 15 minutes, then decorate with pieces of marmalade peel.
Makes 30
Cooking time 15 minutes
Temperature 400°F., 200°C., Gas Mark 6

BUTTER ICING

IMPERIAL	AMERICAN
4 oz. butter	½ cup butter
8 oz. icing sugar	2 cups sifted confectioners' sugar
flavouring	flavoring

Cream the butter in the mixer bowl until white and fluffy, sieve the icing sugar and add to the butter, beat with the mixer until well blended. Beat in the flavouring as required.

Variations

Orange butter icing Add 2 tablespoons orange juice and a little grated orange rind.
Lemon butter icing Add 2 tablespoons lemon juice and a little grated lemon rind.
Coffee butter icing Add 1 tablespoon instant coffee blended with 2 tablespoons boiling water.
Chocolate butter icing Add 2 tablespoons cocoa blended with 2 tablespoons boiling water.
Mocha butter icing Use both the coffee and chocolate flavourings together, with just a half quantity of each.

FONDANT ICING

IMPERIAL	AMERICAN
1 lb. icing sugar	3½ cups sifted confectioners' sugar
1 large egg white	1 large egg white
2 tablespoons liquid glucose	3 tablespoons liquid glucose

Place all the ingredients in the mixer bowl and beat until the mixture is well blended together and forms a 'dough'-like lump, leaving the sides of the bowl clean. Turn out onto a board, lightly sprinkled with icing sugar, and knead until soft and pliable. If you intend to colour the icing, knead in a few drops of colouring at the beginning of kneading. This icing is applied as almond paste in that it is rolled and cut to fit the cake.

ROYAL ICING

IMPERIAL	AMERICAN
3 egg whites	3 egg whites
juice of 1 lemon, strained	juice of 1 lemon, strained
1½ lb. icing sugar	5½ cups sifted confectioners' sugar
1 teaspoon glycerine	1 teaspoon glycerine

Place the egg whites in the mixer bowl and beat on high speed for about 30 seconds. Gradually beat in the sieved icing sugar and lemon juice until the mixture stands in soft peaks. Add the glycerine to prevent the icing from becoming too hard. If you intend to pipe with the icing a little more icing sugar will be needed.

ALMOND PASTE

IMPERIAL	AMERICAN
8 oz. ground almonds	2 cups ground almonds
10 oz. icing sugar	2¼ cups sifted confectioners' sugar
1 egg white	1 egg white
2 teaspoons orange flower water	2 teaspoons orange flower water
few drops lemon juice	few drops lemon juice

Mix together the almonds and sugar in the mixer bowl, add the remaining ingredients, and, using the mixer on a slow speed, blend until a smooth paste is obtained.

Meringue

This is a mixture of egg white and sugar which can be cooked by itself shaped as shells, rounds, or baskets, or used as a topping on puddings.

 MERINGUE 1
(SUISSE)

This mixture is usually used for meringue shells which are filled with whipped cream, or as a topping for pies.

IMPERIAL	AMERICAN
4 egg whites	4 egg whites
8 oz. castor sugar	1 cup sugar
½ pint double cream	1¼ cups whipping cream

Preheat the oven to 250°F., 130°C., Gas Mark ½. Prepare two baking sheets by brushing with oil and then dredging with flour. Alternatively line the baking sheets with non-stick silicone paper. Put the egg whites in the mixer bowl and beat until quite stiff, the mixture should stand up in peaks. Whisk in 4 teaspoons sugar until the mixture becomes more glossy. Sprinkle the remaining sugar into the mixture and fold in with a metal spoon. Shape the meringue mixture into shells with two spoons and place on a prepared baking sheet. For a more professional finish put the meringue mixture into a piping bag with a plain nozzle and pipe into rounds. Dredge with castor sugar and bake in the oven for about 1 hour, changing the trays round to avoid the meringues becoming brown.

After about 1 hour the meringues will be set; lift them gently from the trays with a palette knife, press the flat bottom to form a hollow, then return to the oven to dry for a further 15 to 20 minutes. Cool on a wire rack. Fill with whipped cream and sandwich together in pairs just before serving.
Makes 12–16
Cooking time 1 hour 20 minutes
Temperature 250°F., 130°C., Gas Mark ½

Piping meringue rounds

Piping the walls of a basket

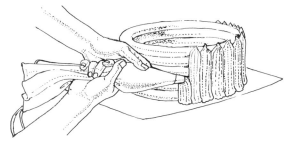

Vertical piping to complete the wall

 MERINGUE 2
(CUITE)

This is a firmer type of meringue which is hard work to make by hand but is quickly done with the mixer. It is really easier to handle than the softer mixture and even an inexperienced cook will find it easy to pipe as it holds firm for longer even in a warm kitchen.

IMPERIAL	AMERICAN
4 egg whites	4 egg whites
8½ oz. icing sugar	2 cups sifted confectioners' sugar
2 drops vanilla essence	2 drops vanilla extract

Preheat the oven to 250°F., 130°C., Gas Mark ½. Put the egg whites in the mixer bowl and whisk until foaming but not quite stiff. Add the icing sugar 1 tablespoon at a time until the mixture is stiff and shiny. To test lift a little mixture up and if ready it should retain its shape as it falls back onto the mixture. Put the mixture into a piping bag with a large plain pipe and pipe as shown in the drawing into 6 baskets. Bake in the oven for about 50 minutes. Alternatively pipe into a large basket. Fill with fruit and cream or ice cream and fruit and serve as a dessert.
Makes 6 small baskets or 1 large
Cooking time 50–60 minutes
Temperature 250°F., 130°C., Gas Mark ½

Note: The meringue takes some time to become thick so do not be worried if it seems to look runny. I find it takes about 5 minutes in my large mixer using a whisk.

HAZELNUT MERINGUE GATEAU

IMPERIAL	AMERICAN
4 egg whites	4 egg whites
9 oz. castor sugar	1 cup plus 2 tablespoons sugar
	pinch baking soda
4 oz. hazelnuts	¾ cup hazelnuts
½ pint double cream	1¼ cups whipping cream
to decorate:	**to decorate:**
8 hazelnuts	8 hazelnuts

Preheat the oven to 275°F., 140°C., Gas Mark 1. Grease and line two 8-inch sandwich tins with greaseproof paper. Make the meringue as directed for meringue suisse. Put the hazelnuts in the blender and blend until finely chopped. Fold into the meringue mixture after the sugar, divide the mixture between the tins, and bake in the preheated oven for about 60 minutes.

Allow to cool and fill with whipped cream which can be flavoured with a few drops of vanilla essence or brandy. Decorate the top with piped cream rosettes topped with a hazelnut.
Serves 6   *Cooking time* 60 minutes
Temperature 275°F., 140°C., Gas Mark 1

VACHERIN

IMPERIAL	AMERICAN
4 egg whites	4 egg whites
8 oz. castor sugar	1 cup sugar
filling:	**filling:**
1-lb. can chestnuts	1-lb. can chestnuts
2 tablespoons sugar	3 tablespoons sugar
¼ pint double cream	⅔ cup whipping cream

Preheat the oven to 275°F., 140°C., Gas Mark 1.

Grease two baking sheets and line each with a round of paper 8 inches in diameter. Whisk the egg whites until stiff, add 1 tablespoon of the sugar, and continue whisking until the meringue takes on a more shiny appearance. Fold in the remaining sugar with a metal spoon. Divide the mixture as shown in the pictures and spread over the oiled paper. Alternatively, pipe in a spiral shape with a piping bag and plain nozzle. Bake in the preheated oven for about 1 hour. Do not allow to brown.

Now blend the chestnuts and sugar together, whip the cream, and mix half of the cream with the chestnut mixture. Sandwich the meringue rings together with the chestnut mixture and decorate the top with the remaining whipped cream.
Serves 6   *Cooking time* 1 hour
Temperature 275°F., 140°C., Gas Mark 1

1. Prepare the 8-inch rounds of oiled greaseproof paper. Separate the eggs and put the whites in a bowl. Switch on the mixer at maximum speed and whisk the egg whites until the mixture is white and stands up in stiff peaks. To test – whites will remain in the bowl when it is tipped upside down.

2. Spread the meringue onto the prepared oiled greaseproof paper. Bake as directed.

3. Here is the finished vacherin with the chestnut purée sandwiched between the layers. It is delicious as a special party sweet.

Eating for health and beauty

Nearly all of us decide at some time to go on a diet. This is usually brought about by discovering that one's dress size has gone up one or the favourite trousers no longer fasten. It is depressing to have a weight problem and it should be tackled at once – the longer you keep it the more it seems to become! Sensible slimming for healthy adults means cutting down the intake of food overall, and making sure you eat plenty of proteins and less starch. If you are eating 2500 calories a day and you are putting on weight this means the body is unable to use all the calories and is storing the excess as fat. No amount of machines or exercises will alter this fact radically.

The blender takes the sweat out of preparing many low-calorie dishes. Fresh vegetables and fruit not only help one to slim but give a bonus of a clearer skin and brighter eyes. Don't be caught napping next holiday time, stay trim by having a low-calorie day once or twice a week. These recipes are also helpful if you are entertaining.

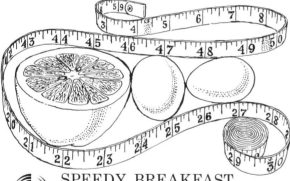

 ## SPEEDY BREAKFAST IN A GLASS

IMPERIAL	AMERICAN
2 eggs	2 eggs
½ pint chilled orange juice	1¼ cups chilled orange juice
2 tablespoons powdered milk	3 tablespoons powdered milk
artificial sweetener to taste	artificial sweetener to taste

Put the eggs, orange juice (frozen juice is excellent), and milk powder in the goblet. Turn on at maximum speed until the milk powder is dissolved. Add sweetener to taste.
Serves 2

 ## YOGURT SOUP

IMPERIAL	AMERICAN
rind of ¼ lemon	rind of ¼ lemon
2 tablespoons lemon juice	3 tablespoons lemon juice
1½ tablespoons sugar or equivalent artificial sweetener	2 tablespoons sugar or equivalent artificial sweetener
2 cartons low fat natural yogurt	2 cups low fat unflavored yogurt
1 egg	1 egg
pinch cinnamon	pinch cinnamon
pinch salt	pinch salt
2 oz. seedless raisins	⅓ cup seedless raisins

Put the lemon rind and juice into the goblet and blend until the rind is finely chopped. Add the sugar and half the yogurt, switch on for a few seconds. Add the remaining ingredients and run the machine until the raisins are roughly chopped. Chill thoroughly before serving.
Serves 4

 ## GAZPACHO

IMPERIAL	AMERICAN
1 clove garlic	1 clove garlic
1 small onion	1 small onion
5 large tomatoes	5 large tomatoes
½ cucumber	½ cucumber
2 green peppers or 1 green and 1 red	2 green sweet peppers or 1 green and 1 red
1 slice white bread	1 slice white bread
1 tablespoon salad oil	1 tablespoon salad oil
1 tablespoon wine vinegar	1 tablespoon wine vinegar
several sprigs parsley	several sprigs parsley
1 pint water	2½ cups water
to garnish:	**to garnish:**
1 dish diced green or red pepper	1 dish diced green or red sweet pepper
1 small dish diced cucumber	1 small dish diced cucumber

Peel the garlic, onion, tomatoes, and cucumber and chop roughly, then put into the blender, switch on, and allow the vegetables to be chopped finely. Add

the roughly chopped peppers gradually while the blender is running at medium speed. Add all remaining ingredients except the water and mix well. Add as much water as the blender will take and mix thoroughly, transfer to a bowl, and chill well before serving.
Serves 4–6

 CHEESE SOUP

IMPERIAL	AMERICAN
2 onions or	2 onions or
4 spring onions	4 scallions
1 large carrot	1 large carrot
3 stalks celery	3 stalks celery
$\frac{1}{2}$ pint chicken stock	$1\frac{1}{4}$ cups chicken stock
8 oz. processed cheese	2 cups shredded processed cheese
1 oz. flour	$\frac{1}{4}$ cup all-purpose flour
salt and pepper	salt and pepper
$1\frac{1}{2}$ pints milk	$3\frac{3}{4}$ cups milk

Chop the onions, carrot, and celery finely in the blender with some of the stock. Pour into a saucepan and add the remaining stock. Simmer for about 10 minutes. Meanwhile wash and dry the blender. Grate the cheese in the blender, putting in cubes a few at a time. Add the flour, seasoning, and half the milk to the grated cheese and run for a few seconds on high speed. Add the contents of the blender to the vegetables, stirring all the time until the mixture begins to thicken. Lower the heat and add the remaining milk. Serve immediately, garnished with chopped parsley and croûtons. This soup is an ideal nourishing lunch-time snack. Use skim milk if you are on a strict diet.
Serves 6–8

 CAULIFLOWER FLUFF

IMPERIAL	AMERICAN
1 cauliflower	1 cauliflower
1 onion	1 onion
2 oz. butter	$\frac{1}{4}$ cup butter
2 tomatoes	2 tomatoes
$\frac{1}{2}$ quantity white sauce (see page 18)	$\frac{1}{2}$ quantity white sauce (see page 18)
4 oz. grated cheese	1 cup grated cheese
salt and pepper	salt and pepper
4 eggs	4 eggs

Divide the cauliflower into sprigs and put into boiling salted water for about 7 minutes. Peel and slice the onion and sauté in the melted butter. Peel and slice the tomatoes, add to the onion, and allow to sauté for about 3 minutes. Make up the white sauce and add half the grated cheese, season well. Drain the cauliflower, arrange in a fireproof dish and cover with the onion and tomato mixture, and top with the sauce. Separate the eggs and beat the whites stiffly with the mixer. Spread the egg white on top of the cauliflower, make four little holes in the white, and drop the yolks into the holes. Sprinkle with the remaining cheese, season again, and grill until golden brown.
Serves 4

 DESERT ISLAND SALAD

IMPERIAL	AMERICAN
12 dates	12 dates
2 tablespoons desiccated coconut	3 tablespoons shredded coconut
rind of $\frac{1}{4}$ orange	rind of $\frac{1}{4}$ orange
1 piece crystallised ginger	1 piece candied ginger
3 oranges	3 oranges
1 banana	1 banana
2 oz. seedless grapes	1 cup seedless grapes
lettuce	lettuce
to garnish:	**to garnish:**
4 slices orange	4 slices orange

Put the stoned dates, coconut, orange rind, and ginger into the blender, switch on at maximum speed for 10 seconds. Peel and slice the oranges and banana, add to the blender, and switch on until the fruit is really finely chopped. Add the whole grapes and serve on crisp lettuce leaves, garnished with slices of orange.
Serves 3

Note: This salad is delicious with roast duck.

STUFFED PEAR SALAD

IMPERIAL	AMERICAN
2 tablespoons blender mayonnaise (see page 17)	3 tablespoons blender mayonnaise (see page 17)
8 oz. cream cheese	1 cup cream cheese
½ slice lemon	½ slice lemon
2 tablespoons milk	3 tablespoons milk
4 ripe pears	4 ripe pears
lettuce or endive	lettuce or curly endive
lemon juice	lemon juice
2 oz. chopped nuts	½ cup chopped nuts

Put the mayonnaise, cream cheese, lemon, and milk in the blender and switch on for about 30 seconds until smooth. Peel and halve the pears and arrange on salad greens which have been sprinkled with lemon juice. Fill the centre of the pears with the cream cheese mixture and sprinkle with chopped nuts. The nuts can be chopped in the blender.
Serves 4

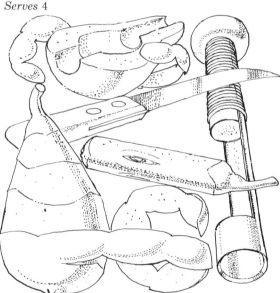

SLIMMERS' LUNCH

IMPERIAL	AMERICAN
1 carrot	1 carrot
1 tomato	1 tomato
6 sprigs cauliflower	6 sprigs cauliflower
6 slices cucumber	6 slices cucumber
slimmers' dressing (see page 73)	slimmers' dressing (see page 73)

Cut the carrot into sticks and the tomato into wedges, arrange the vegetables around the dressing.
Serves 1

CHINESE VEGETABLES

IMPERIAL	AMERICAN
3 tablespoons oil	¼ cup oil
4 stalks celery	4 stalks celery
½ small cabbage	½ small cabbage
2 large onions	2 large onions
2 carrots	2 carrots
¼ pint vegetable stock or water	⅔ cup vegetable stock or water
2 teaspoons soy sauce	2 teaspoons soy sauce
1½ tablespoons cornflour	2 tablespoons cornstarch
4 tablespoons stock or water	⅓ cup stock or water
salt and pepper	salt and pepper
4 oz. bean sprouts	2 cups bean sprouts

Put the oil in a pan. Roughly chop all the vegetables except the bean sprouts in the blender a few at a time—*do not liquidise.* Add the vegetables to the heated oil and sauté for about 5 minutes. Pour in the stock and bring to the boil, simmer for a further 5 minutes. Blend the soy sauce, cornstarch, 4 tablespoons stock, and seasoning until smooth and pour over the vegetables. Season and cook for a further few minutes, stirring from time to time. Add the bean sprouts and continue cooking until they are hot. This can be served with rice or noodles to non-dieters.
Serves 4

TOMATO MOULD

IMPERIAL	AMERICAN
½ pint tomato juice	1¼ cups tomato juice
½ oz. gelatine	2 envelopes gelatin
2 thin slices unpeeled lemon	2 thin slices unpeeled lemon
1 tablespoon lemon juice	1 tablespoon lemon juice
2 tablespoons tomato purée	3 tablespoons tomato paste
1 slice onion	1 slice onion
½ medium-sized cucumber	½ medium-sized cucumber
1 tomato	1 small tomato
1 teaspoon vinegar	1 teaspoon vinegar
salt	salt
lettuce	lettuce

Heat half the tomato juice and put into the blender with the gelatine for about 10 seconds. Add lemon pieces, juice, tomato purée, and onion, switch on until finely chopped. Add remaining ingredients and blend until all ingredients are liquidised. Allow to cool until the mixture starts to thicken then pour

into a 2-pint oiled mould and chill until firm. Unmould onto a bed of shredded lettuce. Serve with tuna, salmon, lean meat, or cottage cheese.
Serves 4–6

WHEAT GERM NUT LOAF

IMPERIAL	AMERICAN
6 oz. pecan nuts	1½ cups pecans
2 stalks celery	2 stalks celery
1 carrot	1 carrot
⅗ pint milk	1½ cups milk
½ onion	½ onion
3 eggs	3 eggs
1½ oz. plain flour	⅓ cup all-purpose flour
1½ teaspoons salt	1½ teaspoons salt
pepper	pepper
4 oz. grated cheese	1 cup shredded cheese
3½ oz. wheat germ	¾ cup wheat germ

Preheat the oven to 350°F., 180°C., Gas Mark 4. Line a 2-lb. loaf tin with greased aluminium foil.

Blend the nuts until chopped, pour into a bowl. Put the roughly chopped celery in the blender and chop, empty into a saucepan. Next chop the carrot roughly and turn into the saucepan. Put the milk, onion, eggs, flour, salt, and pepper into the blender and switch on for several seconds. Pour the smooth mixture on top of the celery and carrot and cook on a low heat until the mixture thickens. Add the cheese, pecans, and wheat germ, mix well. Pour into the loaf tin and cook for about 50 minutes. Allow to cool for several minutes before removing from the tin. Serve with salad and cheese and pineapple dip (see page 8).
Serves 6
Cooking time 50 minutes
Temperature 350°F., 180°C., Gas Mark 4

SLIMMERS' DRESSING

IMPERIAL	AMERICAN
4 oz. cottage cheese	½ cup cottage cheese
½ onion	½ onion
2 tablespoons lemon juice	3 tablespoons lemon juice
salt and pepper	salt and pepper
¼ pint skimmed milk	⅔ cup skimmed milk

Put all the ingredients into the blender and run until the onion is finely chopped and mixture is well blended. Use as a salad dressing and as a dip for raw vegetables.

SOUR CREAM DRESSING

IMPERIAL	AMERICAN
¼ pint sour cream	⅔ cup sour cream
1 tablespoon lemon juice	1 tablespoon lemon juice
2 tablespoons mayonnaise (see page 17)	3 tablespoons mayonnaise (see page 17)
pinch dry mustard	pinch dry mustard
pinch cayenne pepper	pinch cayenne pepper
salt	salt
1 teaspoon dill	1 teaspoon dill

Put all ingredients in the blender, switch on to medium speed until everything is mixed. Chill before use.

This dressing is delicious on a tomato salad or with a fish salad.

FROSTED COFFEE

IMPERIAL	AMERICAN
2 teaspoons instant coffee	2 teaspoons instant coffee
2 drops vanilla essence	2 drops vanilla extract
3 ice cubes	3 ice cubes
⅓ pint cold water	¾ cup cold water
2 tablespoons non fat powdered milk	3 tablespoons non fat powdered milk
artificial sweetener to taste	artificial sweetener to taste

Put all the ingredients into the blender and switch on at medium speed until the mixture is smooth and the ice is crushed.
Serves 2

SLIMMERS' COCKTAIL

IMPERIAL	AMERICAN
rind of ½ lemon or lime	rind of ½ lemon or lime
4 tablespoons fresh lemon or lime juice	⅓ cup lemon or lime juice
6 ice cubes	6 ice cubes
¼ pint cold water	⅔ cup cold water
artificial sweetener to taste	artificial sweetener to taste

Put the lemon rind and juice in the goblet and blend until finely chopped. Add the ice cubes and switch on until finely crushed; pour into glasses and add sweetener to taste. This is a refreshing drink and a change from reduced calorie soft drinks, and when the diet is serious it is better than nothing!
Serves 2

For babies and children

I know that it is easier and quicker to open a convenient little can or jar for junior but it is extravagant on the days when you are having food which is easily made suitable for the baby by blending. It also means the baby is used to family meals and flavours. Many mothers wonder why toddlers refuse food when they are old enough to join the family for meals. Usually this can be traced back to only eating prepared baby foods. It is easy to introduce new flavours with the blender because familiar and favourite flavours can be mixed with new ingredients. It saves money to blend one's own baby foods and this is important to most people now—after all one pays quite a lot for those glass jars!

For older children the blender makes light work of sandwich fillings for lunch boxes, tea time, and parties, and helps you make speedy puddings.

 VEGETABLES, MEAT, OR POULTRY FOR A BABY

IMPERIAL	AMERICAN
3 tablespoons milk or stock	¼ cup milk or stock
4 oz. cooked drained vegetables, meat, or chicken	½ cup cooked drained vegetables, meat, or chicken
pinch salt	pinch salt

Make sure the knife, board, and blender are spotless. Cut the meat into ½-inch cubes, put all ingredients into the blender, and switch on until very smooth. Store unwanted food in a sterilised plastic box until the next day. Do not prepare more than 2 days' food. For toddlers, make a coarser texture.
Serves 2

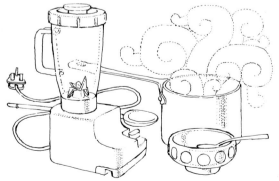

 CHICKEN SAVOURY FOR TODDLERS

IMPERIAL	AMERICAN
4 oz. diced cooked chicken	½ cup diced cooked chicken
1 tablespoon cooked vegetables	1 tablespoon cooked vegetables
1½ oz. cooked rice or potato	¼ cup cooked rice or potato

Put all ingredients into the blender and blend roughly, do not allow vegetables and chicken to become completely smooth. Season according to child's age. Heat through before serving.
Serves 2

 BEEF DINNER FOR TODDLERS

IMPERIAL	AMERICAN
4 oz. lean cooked beef	½ cup cooked lean beef
2 tablespoons cooked vegetables	3 tablespoons cooked vegetables
1 small potato, cooked	1 small potato, cooked
½ tomato, skinned	½ tomato, skinned
1 tablespoon milk	1 tablespoon milk

Put all ingredients into the blender and blend until correct texture is obtained—smooth for very young children, slightly coarser for toddlers. Heat through.
Serves 2
Note: For older children the above recipes can be made with raw food and then cooked in a covered saucepan until the meat is cooked.

 BANANA DESSERT

IMPERIAL	AMERICAN
1 small banana	1 small banana
3 tablespoons baby cereal	¼ cup baby cereal
3 tablespoons milk or made up baby milk	¼ cup milk or formula

Peel the banana, put all ingredients in the blender, and switch on until smooth.
Serves 1

APRICOT APPLE DESSERT

IMPERIAL	AMERICAN
8 oz. dried apricots	1⅓ cups dried apricots
1 apple	1 apple
2 oz. sugar	¼ cup sugar

Allow apricots to soak for several hours. Put in a saucepan, cover with water, add the sugar, and stew. Peel, core, and roughly chop the apple and add to the apricots for the last 15 minutes. Cooking time will be around 25 to 30 minutes altogether. Allow to cool slightly, turn mixture into the blender, and liquidise until smooth. Divide into portions. ❋ Some may be frozen for future use in small plastic containers or plastic bags. Do not serve frozen.
Serves 6

APPLE CUSTARD

IMPERIAL	AMERICAN
generous ¼ pint hot milk	¾ cup hot milk
½ apple, peeled and cored	½ apple, peeled and cored
1 tablespoon honey	1 tablespoon honey
1 egg	1 egg

Preheat the oven to 325°F., 170°C., Gas Mark 3. Put all ingredients except the egg into the blender and switch on until the apple is liquidised–about 30 seconds. Add the egg and switch on for a few seconds to blend the ingredients well. Pour into three greased ramekin dishes and place in the roasting tin or a casserole quarter-filled with water. Bake in a slow oven for about 40 minutes.
Serves 3
Cooking time 40 minutes
Temperature 325°F., 170°C., Gas Mark 3

RAISIN RICE PUDDING

IMPERIAL	AMERICAN
¼ pint milk	⅔ cup milk
2½ oz. cooked rice	½ cup cooked rice
1 egg	1 egg
2 oz. seedless raisins	⅓ cup seedless raisins

Put all ingredients in the blender until smooth, then bake as for apple custard.
Serves 3

BABY DESSERT

IMPERIAL	AMERICAN
3 tablespoons syrup or fruit juice	¼ cup syrup or fruit juice
4 oz. drained cooked fruit	1 cup drained cooked fruit
1 teaspoon honey	1 teaspoon honey

Make the syrup by dissolving 2 teaspoons sugar in 2 tablespoons water. Put all ingredients into the blender and run until very smooth. Apples, apricots, oranges, bananas, peaches, or blackcurrants are suitable.
Serves 2

SANDWICH FILLINGS

Savoury spread Cut one skinned tomato into portions and put into the blender with 1 oz. (U.S. 2 tablespoons) melted butter and seasoning. Blend on medium speed then drop 4 oz. (U.S. ½ cup) roughly chopped meat (ham, chicken, corned beef, etc.) into the goblet a little at a time. Older children sometimes like a little tomato ketchup for flavour.

Egg and cheese Cream 1 oz. luxury margarine or butter with 2 shelled hard-boiled eggs, 4 oz. (U.S. ½ cup) cream cheese, and seasoning using the hand mixer.

Cheese and tomato Grate 4 oz. (U.S. 1 cup) cheese in the blender, then add 3 peeled and quartered tomatoes, salt, and pepper.

Salmon or tuna spread Blend a 7-oz. can with 1 teaspoon vinegar, salt and pepper, 1 tablespoon tomato purée or ketchup, and ¼–½ peeled thickly sliced cucumber.

Sausage pinwheels For these you need an uncut loaf which is then sliced lengthwise. Remove the crusts and flatten the slices slightly with a rolling pin. Spread with butter or marmite or cheese and tomato spread. Place a cooked sausage at the end of the slice and roll as for a Swiss roll. ❋ The rolls freeze well at this stage. To use cut into slices.

Gherkin pinwheels can be made by spreading the bread with salmon or tuna spread and rolling around 2 gherkins.

JELLY WHIP

IMPERIAL	AMERICAN
1 packet jelly	1 3-oz. package flavored gelatin
1 pint water	2 cups water
1 small can evaporated milk	1 small can evaporated milk

Make up the jelly with 1 pint water which is just under boiling temperature. Stir until dissolved, allow to cool, then pour half of the cool jelly (almost at setting point) into the mixer bowl with the evaporated milk. Whisk until fluffy and thick. Use half the remaining jelly to line a mould as shown in the step-by-step pictures. When the jelly is set pour in the whip mixture, allow to firm up for 10 minutes, then add the remaining jelly in a layer on top. Turn out when set. Any flavour of jelly can be used and the whip can be served on its own or with fruit and cream.

Serves 4–6

Note: The jelly may be made up as in the step-by-step pictures opposite with juice from a can of fruit. Dissolve the jelly in $\frac{1}{4}$ pint (U.S. $\frac{2}{3}$ cup) boiling water, then make up to 1 pint with the fruit juice.

DANISH PUDDING

IMPERIAL	AMERICAN
1 lb. cooking apples	1 lb. cooking apples
6 oz. fresh white bread	6 slices fresh white bread
2 oz. butter	$\frac{1}{4}$ cup butter
1 oz. Demerara sugar	2 tablespoons brown sugar
$\frac{1}{4}$ pint double cream	$\frac{2}{3}$ cup whipping cream

Wipe the apples, remove cores, and cut into slices. Place in a saucepan with a very little water and cook until soft. Place in the blender and run until a smooth purée is obtained. Clean the blender. Make breadcrumbs with the bread and fry in the melted butter until golden, stirring constantly. Add the brown sugar. Sweeten the purée to taste but be careful not to over-sweeten. Put alternating layers of apple and breadcrumbs into a glass dish, ending with a layer of breadcrumbs. Whip the cream and decorate the top of the pudding.

Serves 4

1. Make a raspberry jelly with the juice of a can of raspberries. Pour about an inch of jelly into the bottom of a jelly mould. Allow to set. Reserve a little jelly.

2. When the remainder of the jelly is cold, and just about to set, whip it in the mixer with the evaporated milk. Leave the mixer on a medium speed unless there is a cover on the bowl, as it tends to spray out. As the mixture thickens turn to a high speed and it will become thick and creamy. When whisk trails are left when the machine is stopped the jelly is ready for use.

3. Pour into the mould on top of the set jelly, allow to stand for about 10 minutes in the refrigerator, then finish with a layer of jelly. Turn out when the jelly is set and decorate with cream; serve with raspberries.

Drinks

The blender makes delicious drinks for every occasion from children's milk shakes to sophisticated cocktails. Experiment with your own favourite fruits and flavourings. Crushed ice for your drinks is always available at the flick of a switch.

CHOCOLATE MILK SHAKE

IMPERIAL	AMERICAN
½ pint milk	1¼ cups milk
1 teaspoon sugar	1 teaspoon sugar
3 teaspoons drinking chocolate	3 teaspoons sweetened cocoa

Put all the ingredients in the blender and run on maximum speed for 30 seconds.
Serves 2

Variations

Add 1 scoop ice cream to each glass. Different flavourings for milk drinks can be used for milk shakes. Add 1 tablespoon raspberries or strawberries to a plain milk shake mixture in the blender. This is also delicious with ice cream.

LEMONADE

IMPERIAL	AMERICAN
2 large lemons	2 large lemons
1½ pints cold water	3¾ cups cold water
2 oz. sugar	¼ cup sugar

Wash the lemons. Peel the rind off and put it into the blender. Now peel the white pith away and discard, put the fruit of the whole lemon in the blender. Cut into pieces if using a small machine. Add some of the liquid and the sugar then blend until the fruit is puréed. Strain into a jug and add remaining water; add ice cubes and slices of lemon just before serving.

Variation

Orangeade Use ¾ pint (U.S. scant 2 cups) water to 2 oranges and reduce the sugar, or omit, unless you have a sweet tooth.

TOMATO COCKTAIL

IMPERIAL	AMERICAN
1 lb. ripe tomatoes or 15-oz. can peeled tomatoes	1 lb. ripe tomatoes or 15-oz. can peeled tomatoes
1 stalk celery	1 stalk celery
salt and pepper	salt and pepper
2 teaspoons lemon juice	2 teaspoons lemon juice
1 teaspoon sugar	1 teaspoon sugar

Put all ingredients in the blender and switch on to maximum speed for 30 seconds. Sieve into a saucepan and simmer for a few minutes. Add a few drops of Worcestershire sauce if liked and chill well before serving.
Serves 4

PINEAPPLE APRICOT PUNCH

IMPERIAL	AMERICAN
1 small jar maraschino cherries	1 small jar maraschino cherries
10-oz. can apricots	10-oz. can apricots
3 tablespoons lemon juice	¼ cup lemon juice
1 bottle dry white wine	1 bottle dry white wine
4 pints pineapple juice	5 pints pineapple juice

Put the drained cherries, retaining a few for decoration, and apricots in the blender, add a little apricot juice and lemon juice. Blend until the fruit is liquidised. Mix with the remaining ingredients in a punch bowl. Serve with small ice cubes and cherries floating in the punch.
Serves 30

 ## PINEAPPLE
CIDER CUP
Illustrated on page 63

IMPERIAL	AMERICAN
1 orange	1 orange
1 lemon	1 lemon
12-oz. can pineapple pieces	12-oz. can pineapple tidbits
12 cherries	12 cherries
¼ pint sherry	⅔ cup sherry
1 pint soda water	2½ cups soda water
4 pints cider	5 pints cider
to decorate:	**to decorate:**
maraschino cherries	maraschino cherries
slices of orange	slices of orange

Peel the rind of the orange and lemon very thinly and put in the blender with a little pineapple juice; switch on until the rind is finely chopped. Remove the white pith from the orange and lemon. Cut a few orange slices for decoration and put the remainder of the orange and the lemon into the blender with the pineapple pieces. Switch on at maximum speed and allow to liquidise. Empty into the punch bowl, add the cherries and sherry. Pour in the soda water and cider just before serving. Crush some ice in the blender and add crushed ice to the punch; decorate with slices of orange and maraschino cherries as illustrated on page 63. More cider can be added.
Serves 30

 ## SHERRY OR
BRANDY FLIP

IMPERIAL	AMERICAN
1 egg yolk	1 egg yolk
scant ¼ pint sherry	½ cup sherry
1 teaspoon sugar	1 teaspoon sugar
nutmeg	nutmeg

Put all the ingredients together in the goblet and blend for 10 seconds. Grate some nutmeg on the top. I have an elderly relative who has a small blender only to make the daily flip–she swears it gives her all her zing!
Serves 1

 ## WHISKY
SOUR

A gorgeous summer drink. A measure is your choice!

IMPERIAL	AMERICAN
5 measures whisky	5 measures whiskey
2 measures lemon juice	2 measures lemon juice
2 tablespoons sugar	3 tablespoons sugar
2 ice cubes	2 ice cubes

Blend all ingredients together for about 20 seconds. Strain through a small nylon sieve into a jug or glasses. Garnish with lemon slices and maraschino cherries if desired.
Serves 4

CHAMPAGNE
COCKTAIL

IMPERIAL	AMERICAN
4 ice cubes	4 ice cubes
juice of 1 lemon	juice of 1 lemon
3 drops Angostura bitters	3 drops Angostura bitters
2 measures brandy	2 measures brandy
1 bottle champagne	1 bottle champagne

Put the ice cubes into the blender, pour in the lemon juice, bitters, and brandy, and switch on until the ice is crushed. Strain into glasses and top up with champagne.
Serves 8

Index